KARATE
BASICS

KARATE

BASICS

Robin Rielly

TUTTLE Publishing

Tokyo | Rutland, Vermont | Singapore

Published by Tuttle Publishing, an imprint of Periplus Editions (HK) Ltd.

www.tuttlepublishing.com

Library of Congress Catalog Card Number 200305404
Rielly, Robin L.
    Karate basics / Robin Rielly
            p. cm.
    Includes bibliographical references.
    ISBN 0-8048-3493-8 (pbk.)
      1. Karate
GV1114.3.R53 2003
796.815'3--dc21   2003045821

ISBN 978-0-8048-4589-2
(Previously published as ISBN 978-0-8048-3493-3)

Distributed by:
North America, Latin America,
and Europe
Tuttle Publishing
364 Innovation Drive
North Clarendon, VT 05759-9436
Tel: (802) 773-8930;Fax: (802) 773-6993
info@tuttlepublishing.com
www.tuttlepublishing.com

Japan
Tuttle Publishing
Yaekari Building, 3rd Floor
5-4-12 O–saki, Shinagawa-ku
Tokyo 141-0032
Tel: (03) 5437-0171;Fax: (03) 5437-0755
sales@tuttle.co.jp
www.tuttle.co.jp

Asia Pacific
Berkeley Books Pte. Ltd.
61 Tai Seng Avenue #02-12
Singapore 534167
Tel: (65) 6280-3320
Fax: (65) 6280-6290
inquiries@periplus.com.sg
www.periplus.com.sg

First edition
20 19 18 17   6 5 4 3 2 1   1710RR
Printed in China

TUTTLE PUBLISHING® is a registered trademark of Tuttle Publishing, a division of Periplus Editions (HK) Ltd.

To Meghan Rielly Booth:
May your tree grow tall, your book be published
and your children prosper.

table of contents

KARATE TRAINING in the United States has become as common as many of our traditional sports. Where once people engaged mainly in baseball, basketball, and football, they now enjoy participating in a number of other athletic activities as well. In recent years, soccer has grown tremendously. Interest in karate slowly developed in the second half of the twentieth century and then exploded in the 1970s. Since that time, it has become common to see karate schools in almost every shopping mall. You don't need to look far to find karate offered as a means of self-defense, a sport, and a way of keeping fit.

Because of this great interest in karate training, the would-be karate student is faced with a plethora of schools, styles, and organizations. How do you know which is best? How do you know if you will be learning authentic karate? Will you enroll in a school where the main interest is teaching karate, or will you simply be ripped off by unscrupulous individuals posing as martial arts masters?

The purpose of this book is to help you find an authentic karate school. Schools that teach authentic karate do exist, and many styles are available. Prospective adult students are encouraged to do some serious research prior to enrolling in a school, particularly if there is a contract or large sum of money involved. For parents, research is essential if they are to enroll their children in schools that will actually teach authentic karate, not just collect money.

One of the first questions that prospective students usually ask concerns the many styles of karate that they need to consider. The good news is that the actual style of karate is not as important as it might seem. All traditional karate schools teach the real thing, and if you train diligently under a good instructor, the result will be a greater ability to defend yourself, as well as increased personal development. The task is to find a traditional school and a competent instructor from among the legions of schools and instructors available—many of them nontraditional and less than competent. Don't be discouraged by this situation. Hopefully this book will give you the means to ferret out the good from the bad. Included in the text are the basic ideas of how karate training should progress, the hallmarks of good and bad schools, and information that will make you an informed consumer.

I am familiar with many of the styles and systems mentioned in this book, although I have not practiced most of them. It has been my pleasure to meet and observe many fine instructors who teach various styles. I have always found them to be sincere, genuine people with a supreme dedication to karate.

It will be obvious throughout the book that I practice Shotokan karate. As a result, I have used Shotokan practices as examples in many places. This is not intended to indicate that other styles of karate are not as good; I am simply describing that with which I am most familiar. What has always impressed me the most in meeting with senior instructors of other styles is how close we are in many ways, from our practice techniques to our philosophy. The only difference is that we take slightly different paths to the same goal. It is my wish that you will seek out and find one of these paths.

Finally, I must express my gratitude to my assistant instructors and students in the Kobukan Karate Club for their assistance with this work. Cliff Day, Phil Gatti, Po Yeung, and Ben Primost were most patient in posing for the photographs. Expert proofreading was done by Cliff Day. My wife, Lucille, donated much of her time in assisting with the photography and in proofreading the manuscript also. In spite of the assistance of so many, the final responsibility for accuracy always rests with the author.

Robin L. Rielly
Toms River, N.J.
December 10, 2002

part 1
introduction

KARATE IS A FIGHTING ART of Okinawa and Japan, which was influenced by Chinese techniques during its early development and by Japanese techniques in the twentieth century. The literal meaning of the characters that make up the word karate is "empty hand." This indicates that it is primarily a means of unarmed combat, although some practice of ancient weapons, *kobudo*, exists in many karate systems. The original characters for karate, 唐手 translated as "China hands," were indicative of karate's origins. The characters were changed to 空手 in the twentieth century, as Japan began to influence karate's development.

As practiced throughout the world today, karate is considered an excellent means of self-defense, an exciting sport, and a way to keep one's body in good physical condition. Countless thousands of people have become skilled in the art of karate over the past century and have derived many benefits from its practice.

chapter 1
the history
of karate

K ARATE-LIKE FIGHTING SYSTEMS have existed as long as man has taken up weapons against his fellow men. Greek statues depicting unarmed combat exist from several centuries B.C. Throughout the Far East, these combat techniques became systematized and reached a high degree of development, particularly over the last few centuries.

The myths and traditions connected with the development of early karate-like systems are difficult to verify. Some stories may be true, but oral history is always questionable. However, the origins of what we now call karate probably spread from India to China and then to Okinawa, Japan, and Korea. It should be noted that the Chinese had their own combative arts which, coupled with the newly introduced Indian techniques, formed new fighting systems.

The Chinese term *ch'uan fa* means "fist way." The Shaolin ch'uan fa system has come to be known as kung fu in the West.

According to oral tradition, the Indian warrior class, the *Kshatriya*, practiced an unarmed form of combat known as *vajramushti* as early as 1000 B.C. In time, elements of this art were brought to China and influenced the fighting arts there. The pivotal figure in this transmission was the Indian religious figure Bodhidharma. Bodhidharma was born to the Kshatriya caste in India and studied Mahayana Buddhism. Upon the death of his teacher, he traveled to China about A.D. 520 and visited the court of Emperor Wu in Nanjing. After a brief stay, Bodhidharma traveled to the Shaolin monastery on the mountain of Sung-shan and began teaching Buddhism to the monks. Known as Chan Buddhism in Chinese, or Zen Buddhism in Japanese, the system required lengthy meditation, which left the monks in poor physical condition. To keep them healthy and allow them to maintain their fitness, Bodhidharma began to teach them vajramushti. In this manner, fighting systems and Buddhism became intertwined. Over time, the Shaolin monks became known as skilled fighters, and their system of self-defense was known as *Shaolin ch'uan fa.*

Over the next several centuries, the spread of this ch'uan fa system throughout China was usually connected to the spread of Buddhism. In time, many varieties of ch'uan fa developed, influenced by local geographic and cultural conditions. Some systems stressed the use of kicking techniques, while others relied more on the use of hand techniques. In some, the movements were primarily linear, and in others they were circular. There were schools of ch'uan fa that stressed physical strength, and schools that focused on agility and quick movement. Numerous combinations of these basic elements developed, so that many different styles of Chinese combative arts came into existence.

The next stage of karate development took place on Okinawa. As noted above, the Okinawans had their own fighting system. Known simply as *te*, or "hand," it was influenced by the Chinese forms of fighting over an extended period of time. This may have begun as early as the Tang Dynasty, A.D. 618–906. Most historians are content to trace the origins of Chinese influence to the year 1372, when King Satto of Okinawa entered into a tributary relationship with the Ming Emperor in China. This led to increased interaction between the Okinawans and Chinese. Many Okinawans began to study Chinese martial arts on the mainland and brought their knowledge back to the island. In time, these newly introduced Chinese fighting techniques were combined with the native Okinawan te to produce the antecedents of the modern Okinawan/Japanese karate systems. The development of newer fighting systems on Okinawa continued until the early 1600s. In 1609, the Satsuma clan from southern Japan took control of Okinawa and prohibited the practice of combative systems, in order to keep the populace under control. This led to an underground resistance against the Japanese rulers. Since all weapons had been confiscated, the Okinawans began to use common farm tools, such as the sickle and rice flail, as weapons. Simultaneously an increased emphasis on empty-hand fighting developed.

Shorin is the Japanese pronunciation of the Chinese characters for Shaolin.

Figure 1-1: Naha, Shuri, and Tomari, considered to be the towns where karate developed, in the southwestern coastal area of Okinawa

The secrecy required to practice these arts led to the development of separate schools, usually associated with cities in Okinawa. Thus three major styles developed: Shuri-te, Tomari-te, and Naha-te, each with its own emphasis. The three cities of Shuri, Tomari, and Naha were located near each other in the southwestern part of Okinawa near the coast. Naha-te stressed physical strength and in time became known as Shorei, while Tomari-te and Shuri-te became known as the Shorin school. The karate that we know today underwent its major development on Okinawa beginning around 1700 and generally is considered to have emerged from the Shorei and Shorin traditions.

The first names associated with Okinawan karate date from the early to mid 1700s. Takahara Peichin, Kushanku, and Sakugawa Tode are among the early masters who trained others in the combative arts. Other martial arts experts from China were practicing on Okinawa during that period, but their names have been lost in antiquity. Since karate was practiced in secret, little is known about training in the eighteenth century, but more is known about karate's history and development in the latter part of the nineteenth century, when a number of karate masters became famous. Among them were Sokon Matsumura, Yasutsune Azato, Ankoh Itosu, and Kanryo Higanonna.

Satsuma rule ended in 1872, and Okinawan karate emerged from the secrecy that had surrounded it. The first serious public acknowledgment of the Okinawan art came in 1902, when karate master Ankoh Itosu began to teach karate as a part of the physical education curriculum in the First Middle School. This took place with the encouragement of Shintaro Ogawa, Commissioner of Schools for Kagoshima Prefecture, which included parts of southern Japan and Okinawa. Since this new emphasis on martial arts began during a period of growing militarism in Japan, its acceptance in the school curriculum is understandable.

Funakoshi, an experienced calligrapher, signed his work as Shoto, and in time his school came to be known as the Shotokan. The name was adopted by his students, as Funakoshi never gave a formal name to his style. He simply asserted that he was teaching Okinawan karate.

Karate was introduced to Japan proper in 1922, when Gichin Funakoshi gave a demonstration at the All Japan Athletic Exhibition in Tokyo. The founder of judo, Jigoro Kano, witnessed the demonstration and asked Funakoshi to demonstrate at the Kodokan, which was the headquarters for the sport of judo. This interest on the part of Japanese martial arts practitioners led to a series of demonstrations, and Funakoshi soon decided to remain in Japan to teach karate. Funakoshi had studied primarily under Azato and Itosu of the Shorin tradition, but he was also knowledgeable about Shorei. The karate that he taught combined the strong and fluid elements of both systems.

One of Funakoshi's first students in Japan was Hironori Ohtsuka, a master of Shindo Yoshin Ryu jujitsu, one of Japan's traditional martial arts that focused primarily on unarmed combat. After studying with Funakoshi for a number of years, Ohtsuka combined Funakoshi's karate with jujitsu and founded a new style, or *ryu*, the Wado Ryu system. Still other Okinawan karate masters took up residence in Japan. Just prior to Funakoshi's demonstration in 1921, another well-known karate master, Choki Motobu, moved to Osaka and soon began to teach karate there. Chojun Miyagi, a master of Goju Ryu karate, began teaching his art at Kyoto Imperial University in 1928. Miyagi combined elements of the two major systems, Naha-te and Shuri-te to develop his Goju Ryu style. Among his early students was Gogen Yamaguchi, who became an important figure in Goju Ryu karate in Japan. In 1930, Kenwa Mabuni began teaching karate in Japan as well. He had previously studied under Anko Itosu and Kanryo Higaonna. To name his style, he combined elements of each of his teachers' names and called it Shito Ryu. Thus were founded the four major systems of karate prevalent in Japan today: Shotokan, Wado Ryu, Goju Ryu, and Shito Ryu. Over the past three-quarters of a century, many individuals became skillful through study under these Okinawan masters and founded their own systems or further developed that of their teacher. Other Okinawans went to Japan and introduced additional systems. As a result, there are many "styles" of karate practiced in Japan today, all sharing common antecedents.

Karate Develops Further

Karate training up to the first couple of decades of this century was heavily based on the practice and interpretation of formal exercises known as *kata*. In Japan, as the new art became popular, innovators began to develop new training methods. In the 1920s, many of the schools developed systems of prearranged sparring and then began to use free-sparring as a regular part of training. Many of the early karate groups were centered at the colleges and universities, and they frequently trained together to test their techniques. These sparring matches were usually quite rough, resulting in many injuries.

The four major systems of karate in Japan are Shotokan, Wado Ryu, Goju Ryu, and Shito Ryu.

World War II had a devastating effect on Japanese and Okinawan karate. Many karate schools were destroyed and a number of promising karate instructors killed, but in the aftermath of the war, a new generation of karate men began to reorganize their karate systems. By 1948, students of Funakoshi had organized the Japan Karate Association to further the study of Shotokan. Other groups did likewise, and a renewal of the art took place. The idea of karate as a competitive sport developed at this time. Competitions were organized that aided in the popularization of karate, with various associations holding regional and national championships. Some viewed sports karate as detrimental to the art and refused to add competition karate to their training regimen. This was particularly true on Okinawa.

Karate Comes to the United States

One of the great changes brought about by the war was the occupation of Okinawa, which became a base for United States Army, Marine Corps, Air Force, and Navy units. Many of the Okinawan karate men began to teach these military personnel, as they provided a ready source of income on the devastated island. In some cases, the Okinawans were quite generous in the awarding of black-belt grades to the GIs, and some GIs left the island with high ranks after only a year or two of duty on Okinawa. The result was that many Americans who had only minimal training began to teach Okinawan karate. With the addition of American students, some of the organizations grew so large that most of their training centers (*dojos*) were situated in the United States. Registration of black-belt grades awarded in the United States made a welcome source of income for some Okinawan instructors. Fortunately, many Okinawan instructors retained high standards and did not follow this practice.

Karate received its formal introduction to the United States in the mid 1950s, with the arrival of Tsutomo Oshima, a Shotokan practitioner. Oshima took up residence in Los Angeles and began teaching karate there. A few years later, he returned to Japan and made arrangements for Hidetaka Nishiyama of the Japan Karate Association to fill in for him in Los Angeles. Oshima returned in 1963, and Nishiyama stayed on to establish his own karate organization. In the early 1960s, other karate instructors began to arrive from Japan and Okinawa in order to spread their art. The Japan Karate Association sent Shotokan instructors such as Teruyuki Okazaki, Takayuki Mikami, Masataka Mori,

The word *dojo* is the Japanese term for a karate school.

Hirokazu Kanazawa, Tetsuhiko Asai, Masaaki Ueki, Yutaka Yaguchi, Katsuya Kisaka, and Shigeru Takashina to teach in the United States. Some spent a few years here and returned to Japan or went on to other countries. Others remained and founded regional and national organizations. Japanese Wado Ryu instructor Yoshiaki Ajari, Goju Ryu instructors Gosei and Goshi Yamaguchi, and Shito Ryu instructor Fumio Demura, among others, began teaching their respective styles. They were soon joined by many other Okinawan and Japanese instructors, who helped spread various karate systems.

When Japanese and Okinawan experts arrived in the United States, they found that karate was already being practiced here, as taught by the American servicemen who had been stationed in Japan and Okinawa. In 1959 Peter Urban, who had studied Goju Ryu in Japan, began instructing in the New York City area. In 1960 Anthony Mirakian, who had studied Goju Ryu on Okinawa, began teaching karate in Massachusetts. Shortly thereafter, Maynard Miner, who had studied Shotokan in Tokyo, began to teach in New York City. All over the United States, men who had trained in the Far East began to teach the arts. Many joined forces with the newly arrived Japanese and Okinawan instructors, and the karate movement was under way.

> The three categories of American karate schools are traditional karate, semitraditional karate, and "new art."

For the prospective student of karate, understanding this period in the development of American karate is most important. Some of the American servicemen who trained in the Far East practiced with the more experienced Japanese and Okinawans and continued to learn more and progress. Others, convinced that their year or two of training in Japan or Okinawa qualified them as experts, continued to train on their own, founding schools and organizations. Unfortunately, their knowledge of karate was limited and never developed significantly further. Since they were not linked with any international organizations, they founded their own groups and promoted themselves to higher ranks. In time, some built large organizations and promoted many of their students to black-belt grades. These men, in turn, opened their own schools, sometimes breaking away from their original teachers and forming new organizations and systems. As a result, there are many karate instructors today who are far removed from the source of real knowledge of the art. In many cases, the karate they teach is not authentic, and their understanding of the art is very limited.

Fortunately, however, many excellent karate practitioners have been developed by the Japanese and Okinawan instructors who taught in the United States beginning in the early 1960s. Their students were servicemen, many of whom had trained overseas, as well as others who began their practice here. Collectively, these Americans, Okinawans, and Japanese form the bulk of the traditional karate movement in North America.

Since the emphasis on karate as a traditional art was alien to American culture, authentic karate schools grew slowly in the United States. The offshoot organizations and schools, on the other hand, were not devoted to the tradition of the Japanese arts and were able to alter their approach to appeal to a wider range of individuals. The result is that karate in America today may be divided into three distinct categories: traditional karate, semitraditional karate, and what might be referred to as "new art." This distinction is noted in my first work, *The History of American Karate*, published in 1970. At that time these categories were labeled "classical," "semiclassical," and "new art." The word "traditional" replaces "classical" here, as it has come into regular use. Traditional karate organizations are those practicing karate as close to the original, pure style as possible. Semitraditional schools have a basis in traditional karate, but they do not adhere to the practice of original techniques and standards, and they place a great deal of emphasis on sports competitions. Many of these schools attend a tournament a week, and the focus of their training is to accumulate trophies. Such schools are usually easy to identify, as their windows and showcases house an abundant display of trophies. Within the past two decades, "new art" karate has developed. Although it claims to be karate, it is really not karate at all but a combination of gymnastics, dance, and power contests. It is stage-played in front of large audiences, and takes the form of dance routines, labeled as "kata," performed to the accompaniment of music. Other contests are held in which individuals attempt to break a variety of objects such as concrete patio blocks, wood, or ice. Although traditional karate schools occasionally demonstrate breaking techniques, this is not a part of regular training or the purpose of their training.

chapter 2
the philosophy
of karate

THE NATIVE RELIGION of Japan is Shinto, which holds that the emperor is descended from the Sun Goddess, Amaterasu. During the Kamakura period, A.D. 1185–1333, Zen Buddhism entered Japan and soon became an important element in the life of the samurai. By this time, the samurai class, which had developed during the previous five centuries, had become the ruling class in Japanese society. The austere practice of Zen Buddhism, coupled with an emphasis on experience, fit in ideally with the practice of the martial arts. Zen soon became infused into traditional Japanese culture. Most Japanese arts, from flower arranging and the tea ceremony to martial arts, have a significant Zen influence. In traditional karate training, there was little verbal communication, and students were advised not to ask too many questions, but to seek the answers through continued training. This training method was used initially in the United States, but adaptations to American culture soon changed this practice, and dialogue developed between the student and instructor that went beyond what one might experience in Japan.

The word *dojo kun* is the Japanese term used to describe the set of precepts used to remind practitioners of their training philosophy.

One of the traditions handed down to Japanese karate from the Okinawans is the *dojo kun*. This is a set of precepts designed to remind the practitioner of his goal in karate training. Normally, it is recited at the end of the training session, and many schools will have a copy of the dojo kun on the wall. The precepts of the dojo kun vary from system to system, reflecting a variety of training philosophies. The dojo kun of the Japan Karate Association is listed here with an explanation:

1. Seek perfection of character. This indicates to the practitioner that karate is not about fighting, it is about character development. One should not train to harm others, but rather to develop self-control and self-mastery.
2. Be faithful. A karate practitioner should faithfully follow the teachings of the past masters and attempt to improve his life by following their example.
3. Endeavor. One should train sincerely and to the utmost of his capability.
4. Respect others. In all things, one should show respect for his fellow human beings. This includes karate instructors, as well as fellow practitioners and other people.
5. Refrain from violent behavior. Those who train in karate have capabilities above average when it comes to combat. It is unfair in a civilized world to use karate techniques against others unless one is protecting his life or that of another.

Karate tradition contains many sayings handed down from the past. One of the most important is *karate ni sente nashi*. Literally translated, it means that there is no first attack in karate. Karate is to be used to protect oneself, not to harm others. Therefore, it is not considered proper to attack unless one is being attacked. Do not misunderstand this saying. It does not mean that you must stand idly by as another attacks and injures you before you may respond. When it is obvious that an attack is imminent, you may strike your opponent and beat him to the punch. This is basic common sense. But unless directly threatened, there is no justification for using karate techniques against another.

The dojo kun of the Japan Karate-Do Goju Kai states:

1. We are proud to study the spirit of Goju Ryu.
2. We shall practice courtesy.
3. We shall be quick to seize opportunity.
4. We shall always practice patience.
5. We shall always keep the fighting spirit of karate.

On of the most important karate sayings is *karate ni sente nashi*, which means "there is no first attack in karate."

WHEN INQUIRING about the style of karate that a school teaches, remember that there are a great number of different styles. As noted above, many of these are offshoots of the major systems practiced in Okinawa and Japan. The major systems in Okinawa that follow the Naha tradition are Goju Ryu and Uechi Ryu. Those that follow the Shorin tradition are Shorin Ryu, Matsubayashi Shorin Ryu, and Kobayashi Shorin Ryu. These distinctions came into being in the first half of the twentieth century.

In Japan, the most prevalent systems are Shotokan, Wado Ryu, Goju Ryu, and Shito Ryu; however, other systems such as Kyokushinkai, Chito Ryu, Shudokan, Shorinji Kempo, and Shorin Ryu are also widely practiced. These are all of Okinawan origin, but many of the Japanese organizations have modified them to suit Japanese practice and culture.

It is not uncommon for prospective karate students to ask which style is the best. Long-time practitioners are in general agreement that there is no superior style. All take different paths to the same goal: self-mastery and self-defense. What is most important is that the student find an authentic karate school with a competent instructor. Continued training with a good instructor over a lengthy period of time will lead to karate mastery.

More important than the style you choose is the authenticity of the school and the ability of your teacher..

part 2
getting started

P ART 1 provided a broad overview of the history and practice of karate in the Far East and the United States. Now it is time to turn to a more immediate issue, how to get started on the road to karate proficiency.

Many people begin to consider training in karate after seeing movies or television shows that feature characters performing karate-like combative techniques. In the early 1970s, the first of the Chinese kung fu movies became popular. Kung fu is a term Westerners use to describe Chinese combative systems. Within the space of a month, my club grew from about fifteen to twenty members to nearly one hundred. Children, in particular, are much affected by shows featuring characters such as the Ninja Turtles or the Power Rangers. Although these shows are entertaining, they are not what real karate training

is all about. It is not unusual for small children to ask their parents for karate lessons, thinking that they will be doing the same type of acrobatic movements they see on TV. However, when the reality of authentic karate training sets in, children frequently lose interest and quit, since it fails to meet their unrealistic expectations. Some instructors, in order to make a profit, cater to this fantasy and advertise that they teach "Ninja Turtle" or "Power Ranger" techniques. There is no doubt that new movies and television programs that show combative techniques will become popular, and the same clubs will include them in their advertising. This makes it easier to spot the wrong school, but how do you recognize the right one?

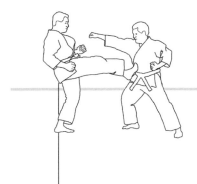

choosing the
right school

INDING A KARATE SCHOOL is a simple matter; however, finding a good one is not quite as easy as it might seem. A brief glance through the Yellow Pages will provide a lengthy list of schools claiming to teach karate. Many will list the names and ranks of their instructors, as well as their qualifications. Others will simply have the name of the school and the phone number. This is where you need to do some research to find an authentic karate school and a competent instructor.

Begin by realizing that a bigger school is not always better. It may simply mean that the instructor in charge is much better at marketing than the others in the area. It may also mean that he has more money to spend on advertising. Obviously, these marketing costs are passed on to the students. Many fine instructors do not have actual storefront schools but teach in rented space in community-owned buildings such as fire houses, church annexes, and the like.

What Is an Authentic Karate School?

Since you are interested in practicing real karate, the first matter to be determined is whether or not the school teaches authentic karate. A few simple questions should reveal if the lineage of the school and instructor can be traced. Where did the instructor train, and who was his teacher? What organization are they affiliated with? Can the roots of the school or organization be linked to Japan or Okinawa, or how far removed are they?

Links to parent groups in the Far East are important, but you should be aware that group politics has caused a variety of organizations to develop there over the years. For instance, the Japan Karate Association (JKA) was the largest Shotokan organization worldwide during the life of its chief instructor,

Masatoshi Nakayama. After his death, many of his senior instructors broke away and formed their own Shotokan organizations, so that now a number of Shotokan groups have emerged from the original JKA. In the same way, many top instructors of the Shito Ryu organization started their own organizations after its founder and chief instructor, Kenwa Mabuni, had passed. Because of this situation, there are now about five major groups practicing Shito Ryu. Each of them has had senior instructors leave, creating additional factions.

The same scenario occurred in the United States. The first of the JKA Shotokan associations established here was the All America Karate Federation, under Shotokan master Hidetaka Nishiyama. Over the years, many of the senior Japanese and American instructors split off and formed their own groups. Today there are a number of excellent karate organizations headed by these instructors, including the International Shotokan Karate Federation, founded by Master Teruyuki Okazaki.

This has been a natural process over the years, with schools of karate forming and training a number of instructors, who then set out on their own and organize their own groups. For the most part, they all teach good karate, and it is simply necessary to trace back the lineage of the senior instructor to discover his roots. This is a part of the process of finding a good karate school, as you will see later in this chapter.

There is a longstanding tradition in karate that one should not profit from teaching it. Unfortunately, in today's economy, this is a difficult tradition to follow.

In chapter 1, the three categories of karate—traditional, semitraditional, and new art—were discussed. What is it you are seeking? If you truly wish to learn karate, then a traditional school is the preferred pathway. However, since the traditional schools normally set high standards for earning their belts and require that their students actually become expert at karate in order to earn rank, they have unfortunately not grown as quickly as those that have lower standards and pass out belts in return for continued tuition payments. As a prospective karate student, you will have to travel a bit or do some hunting to find the real thing. Any small town is bound to have a strip mall containing a karate school. Most will probably be of the semitraditional type. In some cases, the instruction in these schools may be reasonable, and you might actually learn some karate there. In others, you will simply pay a lot of money to an individual who will teach you little, since he has little knowledge himself.

Private Lessons or Group Practice?

In traditional martial arts, one does not take private lessons. You will find that your training will progress faster in a group, where you have many partners to practice with

On occasion, individuals approach our karate school and inquire about taking private lessons. Their thinking is that they will have the undivided attention of the instructor and, as a result, will progress more rapidly. In traditional martial arts, one does not take private lessons. It is necessary to practice techniques against a variety of different attackers, not just one. In the private lesson there is only one attacker to train with, the instructor. As a result, the ability to defend against anyone who does not move like the instructor will be severely limited. Despite the high price for private lessons, the student will not benefit and will actually make less progress than in a class. Training in the middle of a group of enthusiasts who are all chugging along will help motivate you. The same feeling cannot be achieved when it is just you with an instructor. Most instructors who are real karate traditionalists will not give private lessons, so the instructor who suggests that you sign up for them is more interested in making money than in your progress.

Signs of a Good School

Affiliation with a Major Karate Organization

One of the first things to look for is whether or not the school is affiliated with a major international organization, such as the ones mentioned above. This ensures that there are standards for the ranks that the students achieve and that the ranks are recognized by serious martial artists everywhere. Grades issued by such organizations as the International Shotokan Karate Federation, International Traditional Karate Federation, Shito Ryu USA Karate Do Kai, and Goju-Ryu Karate-Do U.S. are widely recognized and respected. The background of the school is where you have to do a bit of research. Many unqualified instructors form organizations of their own with impressive sounding names, but they are little more than facades for their own schools. In some cases, unaffiliated schools group together in an attempt to make their credentials seem legitimate. Fast-buck artists have entered the mix, incorporating organizations that are little more than paper houses. Anyone can send a name and required fees to one of these groups and in return receive rank certificates and titles. When meeting with the school's instructor or representative, try to find out about the organization. How large is it? Where is the headquarters? Who is the chief instructor? Is he affiliated with any international organization, and if so, how? If the answers aren't satisfactory, it is probably a good idea to look elsewhere.

Still another reason for choosing a school that belongs to a large organization is that you may be able to visit other schools and keep up training when traveling. Clubs belonging to the organization will be pleased to have guests. The training will be about the same, and you will have the experience of practicing under a different instructor and with different people.

Sooner or later students will want to test for a grade in karate. In most organizations, the tests for beginner through brown belt are given within the school. Black-belt grades usually require several examiners of high rank. Many of the karate organizations set up regional examining boards that consist of a number of examiners. This ensures a standardization of grades that benefits students, since they will know that their grades have been earned, not bought. A further discussion of the testing procedure will be found later in this book.

Unless he has an injury, the instructor should be able to perform all of the techniques of his art. An instructor who is not that old but is obviously out of shape, or very overweight, is not a good sign.

Competent Instructors

In a good school, instructors are more interested in karate than in making money from teaching it. In a smaller school, the prospective student will have the opportunity to meet with the chief instructor. If he talks about karate and how he teaches it, the genesis of the school, and what you can expect from it, you will probably be in good hands. If his major agenda seems to be how much students pay and how the finances can be worked out, then there is good reason to doubt his motives.

The practice of karate is supposed to be a lifelong endeavor. In time, many of us succumb to the effects of aging and are not able to perform karate techniques quite as well as when we were young, but we still train.

In speaking with the chief instructor, ask him where he trains. In virtually every field of endeavor, professionals are required to continue their education in order to keep up with the latest trends. Most instructors attend special training sessions or training camps with their organization or senior instructors. In this way they can keep up with changes in technique or kata.

An authentic karate school will have a lineage that is easily traced back to Japan or Okinawa. Since karate has only been here for about a half century, it will not take too many steps to get back to its origins in the Far East.

Traditional Classes

A respectable school will allow visitors to watch a class. It should begin with the students meditating and then the instructor and students bowing to each other. Following this should be a period of warming up and stretching. In a general class there will then be three parts: (1) the practice of basic technique, (2) the application of these techniques in sparring drills, and (3) the practice of kata. After the completion of these three parts, there should also be a warm-down period. Many schools will also include some conditioning exercises such as push-ups or sit-ups at the end of the formal session. The end of class is signified by another period of meditation, and the instructor and students again bow to one another. In more advanced classes, there may be a concentration on one of these three parts. A class primarily consisting of black belts may simply do kata or sparring after a short warmup, and not practice basics at all during that session.

The class generally lasts from one to two hours, depending on the level of student skill. Classes with all black belts will usually train longer, since they are in better condition to do the techniques. Even beginners' classes will prove to be tiring for new students, since they will not be in condition to do the techniques.

Classes in traditional schools usually practice in a line, with the instructor counting movements. Between specific drills, students stand at attention and imagine an opponent in front of them. This mind-set helps with concentration.

The movements practiced will be appropriate to the level of the students. For example, beginners will not be practicing jumping kicks or free-sparring.

When you enter the karate school to make your inquiry, you may encounter a number of terms in Japanese that will be confusing. Keep in mind that since karate is of Okinawan/Japanese origin, much of the terminology is in Japanese. For the reader's convenience, a glossary of common Japanese terms is included at the end of the book. Beginners will be exposed to the various Japanese terms during practice. Normally, those taking their first test or two are not required to know them. However, intermediate students are expected to know these terms.

> **W**hen choosing an instructor, keep in mind that one does not achieve high rank at a young age. Instructors in their twenties and thirties who claim to be "grand masters" probably are not recognized outside their own school. Even among top Japanese karate instructors, it is rare to find a "grand master." This seems to be a phenomenon unique to the United States.

Signs of a Bad School
Grand Masters

Karate instructors may have great proficiency in their art, but underneath the *gi* (training uniform) and black belt should be a normal individual. Training in the martial arts is supposed to include perfection of one's character and a certain humility. The instructor who bills himself as a "grand master" is probably very impressed with himself. This is also a likely sign that he has been operating alone for some time, with no one to measure his skill against. Rank is also a gauge for evaluating a school. Later we will discuss the requirements for holding rank in a typical organization.

Business Motives

Karate schools have to pay the bills, which include rent, insurance, utilities, and a host of other items, all of which run up expenses. These expenses have to be passed on to the student. Wherever we go to utilize the service of experts in any field, we expect to pay. This is also the case with karate instruction, but when is the price too high? Instructors who are serious about their karate want others to learn it and practice as much as possible. Their clubs usually charge a flat rate, and the student may attend as many classes as he or she wishes.

They do not usually charge by the class, although some may follow this practice. Normally, dues are paid on a monthly or quarterly basis. Some schools will offer a discount for students who pay a year in advance. Prospective students should be very wary of the long-term contract, however. Contracts suggest that the motive is business more than martial arts. Suppose you find that you don't like practice in the school, or don't like karate practice at all? If you have signed on for a year or more, your contract may be sold to a bank or collection agency, and you may have to pay, even though you no longer train. For adults, a long-term contract may be a poor idea—for children it is insanity. I have raised two children to adulthood and also spent thirty-two years working in public high schools. I know through my own experience that the interests of the young change frequently. What seems like a great idea to an eight-year-old may turn out to be no fun at all when he or she faces the discipline of an authentic karate class. If you are locked into a long-term contract, it will not be to your advantage.

Some schools offer a lifetime membership. This is particularly foolish for anyone to consider. In the case of children, there is no guarantee how long they will be active in karate. Even if they remain for a long time, they may go off to college or move away to work, making it impossible for them to take advantage of the contract. Competition for karate students is fierce today. How do you know that the school will exist a year or two from now? Few karate schools have real longevity, and you would be well advised to look elsewhere if the school suggests that you sign any type of lengthy contract.

Clever marketing has entered the world of karate. Over the years, some individuals have made names for themselves in open competitions. They then begin to franchise their names and build their own organizations. The karate school in which you enroll should teach a traditional art, not one based on the exploits of an individual. This is a business practice and has little relation to the practice of true karate. Such franchises rarely have any real connection to the origins of karate in the Far East, and usually have no international recognition. A number of them have appeared and disappeared over the years.

If the school tries to sell you a program that guarantees you rank, you are in the

Free-sparring is another gauge of a karate school. Some schools have their students free-spar the first night or in the first weeks of training. This is bound to cause needless injuries and lead to really bad technique.

wrong place. As mentioned, we will discuss the specifics of testing for rank later in the book, but we can look at the basics at this point. Testing normally takes place periodically throughout the year. Students perform in front of an examiner and are awarded rank according to their performance on the test and their training record. We have all attended school and recognize that we get out of a class what we put into it. If we didn't study for our math test, we probably didn't pass it. Our teacher had no way of predicting how much we would study or what grade we might achieve on the test or for the course. Why should karate be any different? An instructor can never guarantee the performance of the students. All he can guarantee is that he will do his best to teach them authentic karate. The rest is up to the students. Promises of rank or quick promotion are a bad sign and probably indicate that the school is more interested in profit than in your progress.

Teenagers Used as Instructors

As already noted, I spent many years in public education. During that time, I had the opportunity to work with a number of gifted and talented students. Many were extremely knowledgeable in various academic disciplines such as math and history. However, no matter how great their ability and knowledge of the subject, they did not function as teachers. The idea that a sixteen- or seventeen-year-old could qualify as a schoolteacher would be considered a joke. Why, then, would a karate student of the same age be placed in the position of teaching other students? To be an instructor requires a certain level of maturity and experience that young people simply do not have. The International Shotokan Karate Federation trains instructors in their Instructor Training Institute. One of the basic requirements for acceptance into the program is age. A prospective instructor must be at least twenty-two to be accepted for instructor training. Since the program takes a minimum of two years full-time and several more part-time, a certified instructor would have to be at least twenty-four years of age to be teaching karate. All of the credible karate organizations have similar requirements. Being able to do advanced math does not make a young person a math teacher, nor does proficiency in kicking and punching make one a karate instructor.

Run, Don't Walk, Out the Door

The discussion above has concerned some differences between good and inferior schools. Additional signs of inferiority include (1) the incorporation of free-sparring into the training regimen at too early a stage in the student's training, (2) instructors with an overly mystical style and approach, and (3) the lack of kata application. Some of the schools in existence are so bad that they must be avoided by anyone with any degree of common sense.

Let's try to relate karate training to training in various sports with which most people are familiar, such as baseball. If we go out to the baseball field and watch the team practice, we will notice that they do not simply go out and play a game. Pitchers practice their pitching, and infielders do a number of various drills to sharpen their skills, as do outfielders. Everybody practices batting. After the players have polished a number of individual skills, several practice games help bring the team together. In the same way, students of karate must practice numerous basic skills before they can put them together and free-spar against other practitioners. In many organizations, students may not practice free-sparring until they achieve brown-belt level.

Observe the instructors of the school. As we have previously noted, real karate instructors are normal people with a lot of experience in karate. Occasionally, individuals open schools who do not behave normally. Some of them believe their own advertising and hype, and think of themselves as mystics or believe that they are endowed with some special powers. If, in your conversations with the instructor, his explanations seem a bit too mystical, and his general approach sounds like exotic gobbledygook, this is not the place to enroll. Find an instructor who seems to be a normal person and who can carry on a reasonable conversation.

The backbone of Okinawan/Japanese karate is the kata. As noted previously, in the early part of this century, the kata was the primary form of practice. Woven into the kata are all types of movements, designed to enhance the student's body control and proficiency. A school that does not teach kata is not really a karate school. Any karate practitioner usually knows a number of these forms and understands their place in the karate training regimen. Some unqualified instructors who scorn the use of kata simply do not understand their applications and value.

Lastly, be aware that fads come and go. What is popular in the movies at any given time is Hollywood, not karate. A good karate school will not advertise that their techniques are the same as the entertainment you have viewed on the big screen.

Choosing the right school is the first important step in getting started. Accept the fact that authentic, traditional karate is a serious and difficult endeavor. However, the comradeship with other practitioners and the knowledge gained in learning a complete fighting system, along with self-defense and associated health benefits, will surely outweigh the arduous training.

chapter 5
the karate class

WHEN BEGINNERS ATTEND their first several months of classes, they are sometimes confused by the type of training they must undergo. They may have watched black belts practice various combinations of techniques and engage in free-sparring. Their training, by comparison, seems much less exciting, tedious, and sometimes boring. Why can't a beginner practice advanced techniques? The answer lies in understanding the path to karate mastery. In general, it follows the principle of *Shu-Ha-Ri*, which loosely translates as "obedience-divergence-transcendence." What does this mean?

In the beginning stages of karate training—usually up to and including the first degree of black belt—it is necessary for everyone to learn the basic techniques in a standard way. Promotion to the first degree of black belt indicates that one has a firm foundation in the standard methods of practice. Karate adepts consider first-degree black belt to be a beginner rank, indicating that one has mastered the basics and may now begin to actually learn karate. This is the *Shu* stage, in which one must adhere strictly to the instructor's teachings in order to gain basic competence in technique.

The three stages of karate training are *Shu-Ha-Ri*, which means "obedience-divergence-transcendence."

The second stage of training, *Ha*, is where one begins to adapt the various karate techniques to one's own individual body type. The practitioner is beginning to break away from the standard basic practice. Kata performance during this period begins to change to suit the practitioner. Additionally, a distinct fighting style is developed that demonstrates that the practitioner has learned to adapt karate so that the movements fit his or her own body.

The final stage in karate practice is *Ri*, the stage during which the practitioner begins to make his or her own karate, adopting movements that are appropriate for him or her, but which may not be suitable for any other fighter. Modes of movement that might have been discouraged during early training are now considered acceptable, since the practitioner has the basic foundation to make progress. In this stage, much of the advancement in technique comes not from instruction by others but from introspection, during which the practitioner develops his or her own individual technique to its fullest.

Classes for Women Only

Over the years, a number of women have trained and made significant progress in the practice of karate. There is no shortage of women training and instructing in the martial arts today. Sometimes schools are advertised as teaching women only, with women instructors. Is this a good idea? The average woman who contemplates taking up karate probably is thinking of using it as a self-defense system first and as a sport or other type of exercise second. If that is the case, then it is necessary to train with men and against men, since a woman is more likely to be attacked by a man than by another woman. For eight years, I coached a varsity karate team at a women's college. They were regional champions eight years in a row, and individually the women won many regional and national championships. To a large extent, they had such great success because they were required to train with the regular class at the dojo at least twice a week, in addition to their daily team training at the college. Their experience training against men gave them a great deal of confidence, and this showed when they competed.

Classes for Children

Parents have usually heard that karate stresses discipline and self-development, and that it is ideal for children. This is certainly true, but there are some caveats here. Let's begin with age. It is not infrequent for parents to call our school and ask about enrollment. In many cases, the children are only two, three, or four years old. We politely explain that children of that age are much too young to learn karate. They should be having fun, not getting disciplined. For some, six years of age seems to be a turning point. Children who are six are beginning to have the requisite ability to perform karate techniques, although not all will be ready. This is a developmental issue; some are ready at six, but others will not have the motor skills or self-control until they reach the age of seven or eight. On very rare occasions, a child of four or five may be able to learn, but this is highly unusual.

That having been said, look through the phone book to see if anyone will take children at a younger age. It should come as no surprise that there will be many schools that accept children who can barely walk. We have seen classes advertised for children from one and a half to two years old. They may enjoy the activities provided, but they will not really be learning karate. You will be paying for some expensive baby-sitting.

chapter 6

your first class

ALL RIGHT, you have made your choice, signed the registration forms, and paid your money. Now what will happen? The instructor or the school's staff will have informed you of the hours of practice. You should arrive fifteen to thirty minutes in advance of the class time so that you may change clothes and begin to loosen up a bit prior to the beginning of the formal training session. In a dojo, it is considered unacceptable to be late for class. If you should arrive late for class and must cross the training area in order to get to the changing room, kneel by the side of the training area until the instructor signals you to cross the training floor. Always cross behind the students, never between them and the instructor. Once you have changed into your gi (uniform), you will then be expected to kneel beside the training area until you are told to join in. If this is to be your first class, it would be a poor idea to arrive late, as the instructor would have to take time from other students in order to help you catch up.

During the first few training sessions, it is usually necessary for instructors to spend more time with beginners, since they must learn the techniques before they begin to practice them seriously. Do not try to perform the techniques with any speed when you are beginning; it is much more important to get the form correct. Speed and power will come with training over a period of time.

The word *gi* is the Japanese term used to describe the karate uniform.

Unless you have trained in karate before, you will probably have a few stiff muscles the following day. No matter how good your condition, you will be using your muscles in unfamiliar movements, so some mild soreness is to be expected. A general loosening up and warmup, similar to what you did at the beginning of the karate class, will help alleviate this stiffness.

Children

When we take our children to participate in their activities, we usually like to watch. This is a mutually supportive arrangement, as children like to perform for their parents. In the case of karate, however, it is best if parents do not stay to watch the class, particularly if the children are young or in their first few weeks of training. Children must pay attention to the instructor. Too often, younger children spend much of their time looking to their parents for signs of approval rather than paying attention to the instructor. As they get older, this is not so much of a problem, but for the younger trainees, it is preferable for parents to depart the training area. If the dojo is large enough, it may have a room where parents can wait out of sight of their children. After the child has become accustomed to focusing his or her attention on the instructor, then it should be acceptable to watch the class. If you find that your child constantly looks to you when he or she should be paying attention to the instructor, then you should stop watching practice for a week or two so that the child will stop being distracted.

Training Equipment and Clothing

Equipment

Having enrolled in the school and paid a registration fee and dues, you may be faced with additional expenses. Depending on the school and its requirements, you may be required to purchase uniforms; types of hand, foot, and body protectors; mouthpieces; books; and other types of training equipment. Varied amounts of training equipment may be required, depending on the practice of individual schools. Some may require complete sets of pads, while others use no padding or protective equipment at all. The majority of the traditional schools will not permit the use of padding.

In many cases, equipment is required by the school's insurance carrier. Unfortunately, people are all too ready to sue, in our society, and the threat of lawsuits has had an impact on training procedures in the United States. In order to keep the club running, instructors have to purchase insurance. A

Although traditional karate schools do not permit hand protectors and other types of body padding for practice, they may require some light padding, cups, and mouth protectors for tournaments.

requirement of most insurance companies is that students must wear a large assortment of protective equipment in order to be covered by the policy. This has been one of the effects of having many unqualified individuals running karate schools and not training their students properly. When instructors know what they are doing, their students have a minimal number of injuries.

As long as we are discussing injuries, let's be realistic. If you take part in any type of athletic activity, there is always the possibility of having an accident and getting an injury. For those who have participated in sports before, this is an accepted risk. With competent instruction in a good school, these risks are minimized.

Clothing

Let's begin with the basics, your uniform, the karate gi. Most schools sell their own uniforms, as this helps to pay the bills. However, you may be able to purchase uniforms on the general market as well. Many martial arts suppliers may be found online or through advertisements in magazines. You will find that the cost of a karate gi may run from ten or twenty dollars to between one hundred and two hundred. The difference is in the weight of the uniform and the quality. In general, most traditional schools require a white uniform. Within the past couple of decades, some suppliers have produced gis with different colors, stripes, and varied patterns. However, you will not see these types worn in a traditional karate school. It is normal to have an organizational patch or emblem placed on the uniform, on the left side, over the heart. Some schools, more interested in advertising than tradition, may have their name embroidered or silkscreened across the back. This is not very traditional either, but if you plan to be a member of the school, you will have to go along with its requirements. Traditional schools do not usually do this.

THERE ARE SOME commonsense precautions that are applicable to all athletic endeavors, but some that are particular to the practice of karate. Let's begin with some general precautions. When you participate in an activity such as karate, you should never be under the influence of alcohol or drugs. These will seriously affect your performance, and, if the instructor detects them, you may be banned from the school. Karate training requires that you be in complete control of your body, and people under the influence of drugs or alcohol are not. Use of these habit-forming substances endangers you and your training partners.

Glasses may be worn for the practice of basic techniques, but they would be a danger if worn during sparring practice. If you cannot wear contact lenses, you may be able to obtain safety-type glasses that will not injure you if you are accidentally struck in the face.

Your toenails and fingernails must be kept short. It is impossible to make a strong fist if the nails on your fingers are too long. This is not usually a problem for men as much as it is for women. However, even slightly long nails can cause damage to a sparring partner. Many years ago, I observed the effect that a long nail on a student's big toe can have. In blocking a kick from this individual, his training partner inadvertently used his open hand. The nail on the attacker's big toe cut through the bottom of the middle finger right to the bone, just as if he had used a meat cleaver. It required a trip to the emergency room and eight stitches to close the wound.

Most schools of karate are "no contact." Let's discuss what this actually means. In order to practice safely, we do not actually hit our opponents. Our punches and kicks are stopped short of contact. The greater our expertise, the closer we can come to an opponent's face or body. When we are performing basic drills such as one-step or three-step sparring, this is not difficult with a little practice. When we free-spar, it is much more difficult. This is why students are not allowed to free-spar until around brown-belt level. It takes that long to develop the necessary control. Nevertheless, it should not come as a surprise that people sometimes fail to block properly, or training partners misjudge the distance, and some contact is made. If the school is well run, these incidents are fairly rare, and students understand that a level of trust is required between practitioners in all sparring drills. There will be contact, however, during the blocking procedure. When your opponent kicks or punches at you, you must make contact with the attacking arm or leg in order to practice the block. Some schools allow the use of padding on the arms and legs so that you will not be bruised. This is not a particularly good idea if you are serious about self-defense. If you are attacked on the street, you will not be wearing arm or leg pads. You must get used to the feel of some contact and remain focused; otherwise you will be at a great disadvantage when you try to defend yourself.

Toughening the body and developing spirit are both standard parts of karate training.

part 3

learning
the basics

I N ORDER TO BECOME adept at karate, one must first master the basics. These are the primary techniques that you will use as you progress. It is not necessary to concentrate on the many varieties of basic techniques in your early training; it is more important to master basic movement. Expertise in combinations of techniques will develop over time. First you must learn to use the basic tools. Let us begin our study of karate by identifying the basic techniques to be learned. Please note that we use the term "basic" here because there are many varieties of techniques, particularly when it comes to strikes, kicks, and punches. The term does not imply that these are techniques used only by beginners, but simply that they are major techniques that must be learned as a foundation before varieties of them are attempted.

chapter 8

basic principles

Natural Movement

ET'S CONSIDER a topic that is well known to longtime practitioners but may not seem evident to the beginner. It is the relationship between normal body movement and karate technique. When we first see karate movements, they seem very unnatural to us, since we never use our bodies the way that karate practitioners do. In fact, the idea that there is any relationship between karate movement and our natural movement seems a bit far-fetched. However, a close look at how karate techniques are performed will demonstrate that their connection with natural movements is significant.

Let's identify what we mean by natural body movement—not a difficult task. If you have access to a mirror in the dojo, you can simply watch yourself walk. Look at yourself from a side view and from a front view. Begin by watching your body move forward as you walk toward the mirror. You will notice that your body is straight, not twisted to one side or another. As you walk, the width between your feet will be about the same as that of your hips and shoulders. Your hips will face the direction in which you are moving, and, if you will watch closely, you will notice that they begin to move before your leg or foot does. You will also notice that your body is relaxed and your feeling is centered on the lower half of your body.

Now watch the side view as you walk. Your body will be erect, neither leaning forward nor backward. Again, you will see that your hips initiate your forward movement. Now let's see how this connects with karate movement.

 The most frequently used stance in karate practice is the front stance (see chapter 9, figure 9-1), since most of our movement is to the front or rear. Assume the front stance with your left leg forward. Take one step forward in the front stance. If your movement is in keeping with natural body movement, you should move easily and smoothly. The adherence to natural body movement can be judged in several ways. First of all, your posture should be the same. Your upper body should be straight, as viewed from the front or side. This also means that your hips are in line with your upper body. If your upper body is pitched forward, backward, or to one side, movement will be unnatural and thus slower and more difficult. If you begin your step by leaning forward, this places your hips back, and the movement is again unnatural. Applying this principle to movement in the front stance, the body should also be in an upright position and straight, as viewed from front to side. In normal walking, the sequence of movement in the lower body is hip, leg, and then foot. When we perform the stepping movement in the front stance, the hips must move first. In the ending position for the front stance, the hips are still straight.

 Though the movements in karate may appear awkward or unnatural at first, you'll find that by following your body's natural movement you'll be better able to perform the techniques.

Let's take a simple combination movement in karate to see how hip movement and body posture apply. The practitioner stands in the left front stance with the left hand in the downward block position and the right fist at the hip. He then steps forward and executes a right lunge punch to the face and then a left front kick. If he has moved in accord with his body's natural movement as he performed the lunge punch, his hips will be in the correct position for the kick. If the beginning of the kicking movement is slowed, it is probably because his hips are out of their natural position. The common error here is to lean forward as one punches, angling the hips to the rear and out of position for a smooth transition to the kicking movement.

We can also observe how correct hip and body posture affect complex turning and shifting movements. In many of the kata there are movements that require us to turn anywhere from 90 to 270 degrees. Such movements can only be accomplished smoothly if the body's posture is straight, as it naturally should be. If the hips are out of alignment or the upper body is crooked, movement will be awkward and slower.

Training Technique versus Fighting Technique

To the uninitiated observer, karate movements during basic training sessions seem to be stiff and have little application to fighting. What most do not realize is that they are seeing training activities, not real fighting. Let's think in terms of boxing training. The boxer may practice against the speed bag. Obviously there will be no opponent whose head bobs and swings that rapidly. The boxer is training specific skills, such as rhythm and timing. In the same way, the karate practitioner trains numerous specific skills by using a variety of training methods. No karate fighter begins a match by shifting into the front stance and performing a downward block, as he would in a training drill. The low stances, hands withdrawn to the sides during punches, and like movements are methods of training the body to perfect skills. Training in a low front stance strengthens the legs and gives one the ability to move rapidly forward and backward. This ability will be evident during practice of free fighting, when long movement will give you an advantage over your opponent. As a result of all the varieties of training methods, you will be able to move quickly, with strength and speed. In the middle of a match, the stances are momentary positions used as techniques are executed. No one stands in them. Since the different stances form the basis for all of our other techniques, it is necessary to examine each and to understand its function.

Develop power in your technique by executing:

☞ Correct technique

☞ Correct breathing

☞ Focus

☞ Use of reaction force

Breathing

Breathing correctly is an important part of any karate technique. Our natural breathing patterns must be followed as closely as possible, to maximize the power of our techniques and also to prevent us from tiring rapidly. Normal breathing causes the abdomen to expand and contract, and this type of breathing must be used as we perform karate techniques. When punching, kicking, and blocking, it is important not to hold your breath. It is correct to exhale as the technique is being performed. This allows for maximum contraction of the muscles as the technique is completed, and it is a prerequisite for good focus.

Developing Power in Your Technique

To develop power in technique, it is necessary to perform the technique properly. Karate techniques are quite precise, and maximum power is developed when they are executed correctly. Power comes from a combination of factors, including (1) correct technique, (2) breathing, (3) focus (*kime*), and (4) reaction force. Your instructor will teach you the way to perform the techniques correctly. Take your time and get the movement right, or you will never be able

Karate is not about comparing yourself with others, it is about maximizing your own personal technique.

to develop your maximum power. Breathing, as noted above, must follow a natural pattern, with exhalation accompanying the exertion of a kick, punch, or block. Kime, or focus, refers to the instantaneous tension of all the body muscles and extreme concentration on the target at the moment of impact. This holds true for blocks as well as offensive techniques. Reaction force is a natural component of power. Let's look at how this works in a reverse punch (see chapter 11). Stand in the front stance with the left arm extended in front of your body as if you had just punched. Your right fist, palm upward, is held just above your right hip. Without moving your left arm, punch with your right. Try this several times. Now punch again, simultaneously withdrawing the left arm sharply as you punch with the right. You will notice a big difference in the feel of the punch. You have added reaction force to the technique by withdrawing the left arm sharply. This has caused a reaction in the arm that is doing the punching, and the punch will have more power. Another factor that affects reaction force is the solidity of the stance. When we punch toward a target, the rear foot must be flat on the floor and, at the moment of impact, the leg and its muscles are tensed. This locking of the rear leg causes a reaction force to be transmitted from the rear leg to the punching arm, thus making the punch more powerful.

Connection

When karate instructors speak of connection, they refer to a specific set of circumstances necessary for the karate practitioner to exert maximum power in the performance of technique. Connection implies that the entire body is acting as one unit, with the lower and upper parts of the body working together. If they are not connected in this way, then the power from the legs and hips cannot be transmitted to the arms and hands as they perform blocks, thrusts, and strikes. This capability is greatly dependent on the use of the abdominal muscles, as they form the connective structure between the two halves of the body. If they are loose, as a hand technique is being performed, then it is difficult to transmit the power of the lower body into the technique. If they are tensed at the moment of impact, as the karate practitioner (*karate-ka*) focuses on the target, then the technique will have maximum power. One of the primary ways to develop this connection is through the use of the punching post, or *makiwara*.

The Kiai

A *kiai* is a spirited yell given at the moment a karate technique comes to its conclusion. It is an important part of karate technique, as it helps to focus energy at the moment of impact. It also can have a psychological effect, both on the performer and his or her opponent. During the training session, the instructor will frequently direct the class to kiai at certain times, particularly during sparring drills. When performing a technique, the karate-ka usually exhales. As the exhalation is taking place, a short sound is yelled out to help focus the muscles of the abdomen. This is the kiai.

Karate-ka is the Japanese term used to describe a karate practitioner.

In order to be performed correctly, the kiai must originate in the abdomen, not in the chest or throat. It is essential that the sound be of short duration, in order to have maximum effect. Long, drawn out kiais spread the tension over too great a period of time, and thus it loses its effectiveness.

It is not unusual to hear a beginner yell the word "kiai" when directed to make the sound. This is incorrect. One needs to utter a short, guttural sound, such as "eh" or "toe." Some of the circus types of competitions popular in

A *kiai* is the Japanese term used to describe the martial arts yell.

American culture today have so-called karate experts standing in place and yelling extended kiais at the top of their lungs, with the sound emanating from their throat. This obvious error, coupled with the length of the sound, gives evidence that they and their instructors have no clue as to the correct application of the kiai.

Proper Tension and Relaxation

In order to perform karate movements correctly, one must learn to tense and relax the muscles of the body at the proper time. It is not possible to develop maximum speed or power in technique if the body is stiff. There is no need to keep the body muscles tensed. One must remain relaxed until the actual moment of impact with the opponent. In that split second, we tense everything as we focus. We must then immediately relax our bodies as we follow with another movement, whether it is an attack, defensive movement, or body shift. Failure to immediately relax the body will make it difficult to move quickly to the next position. Tension/relaxation control is one of the more difficult things to learn, and the failure to stay relaxed causes many new students to tire quickly during training. The tendency is usually to keep the body stiff prior to a movement and for too long a period afterward.

Selecting a Target

One cannot simply throw punches and kicks at random—they must be aimed at a vulnerable part of the opponent's body. Imagine being equipped with a gun and simply firing bullets all over the place. You might get lucky and hit the bull's-eye, but probably not. In karate practice, it is always most important to aim at a target on the opponent's body. Being off by an inch or so can mean the difference between victory and defeat. Visualize your target, even during individual practice or in sparring drills, when you do not have an opponent in front of you. That way, there will always be an imaginary opponent facing you in other drills and kata.

You must aim at a specific target on the opponent's body in order to have a chance to stop him. Numerous charts can be purchased from martial arts supply houses, showing the vulnerable parts of the human body. If viewed from the front, the major points are in a straight line down the center of the body, and also along the route of an X, beginning at the temple and going down and across the torso. Starting at the top center of the body, they are: bridge of the nose, eyes, point under the nose just above the upper lip, point of the chin, Adam's apple, solar plexus, pit of the stomach, and groin. Following the frontal X pattern, they are: temple, rear point of the jaw, side neck artery, collarbone, point just under the nipple, soft or cartilage ribs, and, following around the body, the kidneys. From the rear, the points are: top of the spinal column by the neck, backbone between the shoulder blades, kidneys, and tailbone. Additional targets include the side of the knee, the instep, and the Achilles tendon.

Whenever you are practicing, you should aim your attack at the nearest available target. Many of these targets are extremely vulnerable, and great care must be taken so that you do not injure your training partners. Some points are so critical that it is prohibited to aim for them in practice. The eyes, groin, Adam's apple, and knees fall into this category.

In all training matches and sparring drills, caution must be taken. Since traditional karate schools do not usually allow the use of protective padding, it is essential that practitioners have excellent control of their techniques before engaging in free-sparring. That is why it is best to wait until at least brown-belt level before engaging in this type of training.

STANCES ARE NOT UNIQUE to karate; they are used in other combative arts and sports. Fencers have put them to use throughout the ages, and baseball players, when standing at the plate, place their feet and body in the best position to hit the ball, called a batting stance. In karate, stances form the base for the delivery of hand and foot techniques. The relative power of a punch or block is strongly affected by the position of the body as it is delivered. If the stance is solid and well balanced, then the hand technique is strong. If not, it is liable to lack sufficient power to produce the desired effect. Some stances allow rapid shifting forward and rearward, while other stances make sideways movement faster. Others have very specific uses during the performance of attacking or defensive techniques. Stances in themselves are not only used in fighting, they are also excellent methods of building strength as we train. Karate training involves the use

Karate stances will form the basis for all of your techniques and movement, it is necessary to practice them constantly.

of a variety of stances, each with a different purpose. Some of the stances are simply the natural way that we stand, while others are designed to add stability to the body as it performs karate techniques or to add power to the techniques.

Natural Stances

Let us begin with what are known as the natural stances. This group may be divided into two categories: formal stances used to begin a kata or to bow, and

> The natural stances include *heisoku-dachi*, where your feet are together and parallel; *musubi-dachi*, where your heels are together and your feet are turned outward; *heiko-dachi*, where your feet are shoulders' width apart and parallel; *hachiji-dachi*, where your feet are shoulders' width apart and are turned outward; *uchi-hachiji-dachi*, where your feet are shoulders' width apart and turned inward; *teiji-dachi*, the T stance; and *renoji-dachi*, the L stance.

normal stances, which may be seen as regular positions in which the student stands or performs normal movements. At the beginning of a kata or practice drill, students may stand with their feet together, seemingly at attention. There are two types of attention stances. When the feet are parallel, the stance is called *heisoku-dachi*. If the heels are together and the feet turned outward, it is known as *musubi-dachi*. Stances that may be seen as normal, everyday positions are ones in which the feet are about shoulders' width apart. If the feet are parallel, it is called *heiko-dachi*. When they are turned outward, it is known as *hachiji-dachi*, and if turned inward, *uchi-hachiji-dachi*. In the T stance, *teiji-dachi*, the rear foot is turned outward, and the forward foot points straight ahead. A line drawn through the center of the lead foot would bisect the rear foot. If the line through the front foot lines up with the heel of the rear foot, the stance is called the L stance, or *renoji-dachi*. These stances are normally passive stances, in that they are not used in specific karate techniques but as starting points or intermediate positions while performing kata or other karate applications.

> The word *dachi* is the Japanese term used to describe "stances." The karate stances are divided into three categories: natural stances, outward tension stances, and inward tension stances.

Stances for Performance of Techniques

Let's look at stances that are used in the performance of actual karate techniques. They are divided into two groups: those in which the tension on the knees is outward, and those in which the tension on the knees is directed inward. The former are usually learned first and the latter as the student becomes more advanced. Outward tension stances include the front stance, back stance, straddle-leg stance, square stance, and rooted stance. Stances in which the tension on the knees is inward are the cat-foot stance, the hourglass stance, and the half-moon stance. In the explanations that follow, you will notice that a stance is described as being two shoulders' widths, and so on. These descriptions of the distances between the feet are to be considered starting positions. It is understood that there will be some variation from person to person, according to age and body type.

Outward Tension Stances

Front Stance

The front stance, or *zenkutsu-dachi*, is used for basic movement forward and backward. From this stance one may perform a variety of blocks, strikes, punches, and kicks. It is the most common stance in karate. In the front stance the feet are placed about shoulders' width apart as viewed from the front. From the side, the distance between the feet appears to be about twice the width of the shoulders. Sixty percent of the weight of the body is on the front leg and 40 percent on the rear. Tension on the knees is outward. The outside edge of the front foot points directly forward, and

Figure 9-1: Front stance

the rear foot is angled out at about forty-five degrees. This is an average position, and those who are more flexible may be able to point the rear foot forward at a greater angle, while those with stiff ankles may have to point the foot more to the side.

Back Stance

The back stance, or *kokutsu-dachi*, is one in which 70 percent of the weight is carried on the rear leg and 30 percent on the front leg. This stance is particularly useful in dodging an opponent's attack and quickly shifting back toward him to counter. It is possible to do this because there is great tension on the rear leg. When viewed from the side, the distance between the feet is about twice the width of the shoulders. From the front, the outside edge of the front

Figure 9-2: Back stance

Figure 9-3: Straddle stance

foot is in line with the heel of the rear foot. The angle between them is ninety degrees. Normally, during training, students will practice the knife-hand block in this stance.

Straddle Stance

In the straddle stance, or *kibu-dachi*, the weight is evenly distributed on both feet. The feet are placed approximately twice the width of the shoulders apart, and the feet are parallel to one another. Tension is outward on the knees and legs. This stance allows rapid movement to the side and presents less of a target area to the opponent. Since the body is turned to the side and the strongest punches and kicks are generally delivered from the front stance, the body must be shifted in order to perform a technique. This stance is particularly useful in delivering powerful side kicks, as the body is in a perfect position to do so.

Square Stance

The square stance, *shiko-dachi*, resembles the straddle stance in that tension on the knees is also outward. The primary difference is that the feet turn outward at an angel of forty-five degrees and the body is lower. Movement in this stance is difficult, and it is a transition stance for many karate movements. It is also useful in lowering the body to punch at an opponent on the ground, as it makes it much easier to keep the back straight and avoid being pulled down by the opponent.

> The straddle stance is also known as the horse-riding stance, since the legs look as though they could be straddling a horse.

Figure 9-4: Square stance

Figure 9-5: Rooted stance

Rooted Stance

The rooted stance, or *fudo-dachi*, is also known as *sochin-dachi*, since it is the main stance in the kata *Sochin*. In the rooted stance, the weight is evenly distributed on both legs and the body lowered. Tension is exerted outward on the knees. The feet are approximately two shoulders' widths apart when viewed from the side. Both feet are at about a forty-five degree angle to the line of movement. The rooted stance may be thought of as a cross between the front stance and the straddle stance, because a simple change in foot position can allow the performer to shift from a straddle stance to the rooted stance. Movement in this stance is not as rapid as in the front stance or straddle stance, but, because of its low, powerful position, it is ideal for stopping an opponent's charge and delivering a counterblow.

Inward Tension Stances

Let's take a look at the second category of stances, those in which the tension on the knees is inward. Inward tension stances have two advantages over those in which the tension on the knees is outward. First of all, the inward tension requires that the upper legs be closer together, providing additional protection for the groin. The second advantage is that the inward tension allows for better traction on slippery surfaces.

Cat-Foot Stance

The cat-foot stance, or *neko-ashi-dachi*, is particularly useful if one desires to use the front foot for kicking. Since more than 90 percent of the body weight is on

Figure 9-6: Cat-foot stance

Figure 9-7: Hourglass stance

the rear leg, the front knee may be raised quickly to execute a kick. To perform the cat-foot stance, turn your rear foot approximately forty-five degrees forward and lower your body on the rear leg. As you do this, withdraw the lead foot until it is only six to twelve inches in front of the rear heel and rests on the ball of the foot. The heel of the front foot is raised and the knee flexed. The front foot points directly forward. Tension is inward on both knees, and the groin is a difficult target to hit in this stance. One does not normally stand facing an opponent in this stance, since the lack of weight on the front foot makes it easy for the opponent to sweep it. In the course of fighting, one would normally shift into this stance quickly, execute a front leg kick, and then return to another stance or technique.

Hourglass Stance

The hourglass stance, *sanchin-dachi*, is a short stance, with the feet relatively close together. There is equal weight distribution on both feet. In this stance, the heel of the lead foot is only a few inches in front of the toes of the rear foot. The feet are placed about one shoulders' width apart, with the rear foot facing forward and the front foot turned inward. The knees are tensed inward as well. This is a stance

The outward tension stances include *zenkutsu-dachi*, which means "front stance"; *kokutsu-dachi*, which means "back stance"; *kiba-dachi*, which means "straddle stance"; *shiko-dachi*, which means "square stance"; and *fudo-dachi*, which means "rooted stance."

Figure 9-8: Half-moon stance

for close-in fighting, and since the knees and upper legs are flexed inward, the groin is given excellent protection. This may be considered a transitional stance, because the fighter will shift into it and then quickly into another stance.

Half-Moon Stance

The half-moon, or crescent, stance is called *hangetsu-dachi*. It is somewhat similar to the front stance but is not quite as long. The weight is evenly distributed on both feet. The knees are tensed inward and give good protection to the groin area. Both feet turn inward at about forty-five degrees. This stance is used for movement forward and backward, and the feet trace a crescent pattern as the movement is executed. It is seen in the kata *Hangetsu*.

Balance and Stability

The stances described above have particular functions in relation to the execution of karate techniques. They are all designed to provide a stable base for the hand, body, and leg movements that are the techniques of karate. If you have a weak base or stance as you perform a hand technique, it will be impossible to utilize 100 percent of the body's power. Let's consider a few of the factors that contribute to balance and stability.

Stability is dependent upon the size of the base created by spreading the feet apart. Human beings have two legs, so our base will only provide stability in certain directions. Normally we produce maximum stability if our feet are spread about a shoulders' width apart as seen from the front and about twice that distance when seen from the side. Stances in which the feet line up, such as the back stance, or in which the base is quite small, such as the cat-foot stance, are not as stable as the front stance or rooted stance.

Beginning at the extreme bottom of the base, we can look at foot position. The feet must be planted on the floor so that the soles of the feet make maximum contact. If your heel is raised as a punch is delivered, it will not utilize the body's force correctly, and the punch will not be as strong as it might have

The inward tension stances include *neko-ashi-dachi*, which means "cat-foot stance"; *sanchin-dachi*, which means "hourglass stance"; and *hangetsu-dachi*, which means "half-moon stance."

been if your feet had been planted firmly. If your heel or toes are raised off the floor, there is less contact area to support your body, and the result is poorer balance and a diminished ability to transmit power.

A second part of the body that must be considered is the knees. In all of the karate stances, the knees are flexed, not held straight. In the more upright stances this is particularly important because the base is narrowed. The only exception to this rule would be the knee of the rear leg in the front stance.

Similarly, the hips must be lowered. Normally, the lowering of the hips goes along with the flexing of the knees. What is important is that your body must be relaxed so that your feeling is centered in the lower part of your body. Tensing the body tends to bring the feeling up to the chest and shoulders, which works against stability. Lower stances tend to be more stable than higher ones, since the center of gravity is lower.

THERE IS AN INFINITE VARIETY of blocking techniques that you can use in defending against an attack. Both arms and legs may be used in these blocking techniques, with the arms used most frequently. Although some blocks are more useful than others, mastery of many different varieties is necessary if you are going to protect yourself effectively.

Hand Blocks

Let us begin by understanding that there are six basic blocking motions that we perform using our hands. They are: (1) upward, (2) downward, (3) from the outside inward, (4) from the inside outward, (5) straight, and (6) circular. Each will have many variations, depending on which part of the hand or arm is employed in the block.

Rising Block

The rising block, or *age-uke*, may be performed with a variety of hand positions. Normally it is performed with a fist, as shown in Figure 10-1. The rising block is used to deflect a punch aimed at your face in an upward direction. This block is also useful when a strike is aimed at your head from above, such as a blow with a stick. In order to have sufficient strength in this block, your blocking arm must be at about an angle of forty-five degrees, with the hand higher than the elbow. You must take

Figure 10-1: Rising block

care not to have your arm too close to your face, or your opponent's attack may force your blocking arm to strike you. Since the block is designed to deflect a punch upward, the upper edge of your forearm must be above the level of the top of your head.

Begin the right rising block with your right hand held at the side of your body, with the palm upward. Your left arm is already in the left rising block position. Bring your right arm across your body in an upward motion at an angle of about forty-five degrees. Rotate your hand as the block travels upward so that the thumb is down in the ending position. Simultaneously bring your left hand sharply to the left side, with the palm upward. Your blocking arm has traced a path to the outside of the withdrawing arm.

Figure 10-2: Downward block

Downward Block

The downward block, or *gedan-barai*, is probably the most frequently used block in karate (Figure 10-2). It is used to deflect a kick or punch away from the lower part of your body. The movement for this block is downward and outward so that the kick or punch is deflected to the outside of your body. The block begins with your fist held against the opposite side of your head, palm inward near the temple. The other arm is held straight downward, pointing toward the center line of your body. The blocking arm is on the outside. To perform the block, sweep the blocking arm down to a point where its outside edge is in line

The six basic blocking motions performed with the hands are:

☞ Upward

☞ Downward

☞ From the outside inward

☞ From the inside outward

☞ Straight

☞ Circular

with the side of your body. In the front stance, there is a distance about the width of two fists between the hand and the leg when the block is completed. If your blocking arm is held farther out from your body, a kick may pass underneath it. If it is held too close, it may be forced into your body by the kick. The reverse of this block is known as *gaiwan-gedan-uke*. Used against lower attacks, this movement is done with your arm straight and in a position similar to that of the downward block. The straightened arm is swung across the lower section of your body from outside to inside, making it one of the blocks using the outside-to-inside movement.

Outside Block

The outside block, known as *chudan-ude-uke* or *soto-uke*, travels from the outside of the body inward and across the body (Figure 10-3). It is used to deflect an attack to the midsection. To perform the block, begin with your blocking hand held high and to the outside of your body, with your fist about level with the top of your head. Swing it downward and across your body, deflecting an attack to the lower face or the middle of the body. In the ending position, your elbow is approximately one fist's distance from your ribs, your arm is bent at about ninety degrees, and your fist is level with your shoulder. The blocking edge of your arm lines up with the side of your body. It may also be used to

Figure 10-3: Outside block

Figure 10-4: Inside block

deflect an attack to the head. Among the variations of this block are those using the knife-hand and open hand.

Inside Block

The inside forearm block is known as *uchi uke (Figure 10-4)*. It is used primarily to deflect attacks to the midsection, although variations are also used to block attacks to the head. To perform the inside block, begin with your blocking hand under your opposite armpit, with your palm facing downward. Snap your arm outward, using your elbow as a pivot. The ending position of this block is similar to that of the outside block—that is, your elbow is approximately one fist's distance from the ribs, your arm is bent at about ninety degrees, and your fist is level with the shoulder.

Knife-Hand Block

The knife-hand block, or *shuto-uke*, uses the outer edge of the hand to block the opponent's arm (Figure 10-5). To perform the knife-hand block, begin with your blocking hand held in the knife-hand position against your opposite ear. Your other arm is placed palm down in front of your body. Snap your blocking hand downward and across your body, deflecting your opponent's punch to the

Figure 10-5: Knife-hand block

Figure 10-6: Circular block

outside of your body. Your blocking hand travels in a relatively straight line to your opponent's arm. Your opposite hand is withdrawn to a position just under your solar plexus, with your palm up in the four-finger spear-hand position. This block is frequently performed in the back stance during training, but any stance may be used.

A block consists of three parts: the movement of the arm, the rotation of the body, and a shifting of the body.

Circular Block

The circular hooking block, or *mawashi-kake-uke*, utilizes a circular movement of the hands to deflect the opponent's attack to the outside of the body (Figure 10-6). One hand is held in the *jodan*, or upper blocking, position, and the other near the midsection. Both are rotated in a circular movement in front of the body, hooking the opponent's attacking arm and deflecting it downward and outward from the body. It is seen in the kata *Nijushiho*.

To perform the circular block, begin with your left hand in the same position as for a rising block, with the hand open and the palm forward. Your other hand is held open in front of the lower-middle part of your abdomen. Rotate both arms in a circular, clockwise position, hooking your opponent's wrist as he punches or grabs at you. This may be done clockwise or counterclockwise.

We have discussed the six basic blocking motions in the preceding paragraphs. Any block that we perform in fighting has to be one of these, or a variety of one. For instance, the rising block, age-uke, may be performed with the hand held in the knife-hand position and is then called *age-shuto-uke*. If the hand is held open and bent downward so that the top of the wrist contacts the opponent's punching arm, then the block is known as the bent-wrist block, or *kakuto-uke*. Still other variations of the rising block are the rising palm-heel block, *age-teisho-uke*; the two-handed X block with the hands open or held in fists, *age-juji-uke*; and the chicken-head wrist block, or *keito-uke*. In this way, each of the six basic blocking motions gives rise to a number of other blocks utilizing various parts of the hand and wrist.

The blocks described above have focused on the use of the arm. It must be noted, however, that blocking movements usually include three parts. The first is the movement of the arm, as described above. The second involves rotation of the body. In the case of attacks to the midsection, this is extremely important, as the side-facing position presents less of a target. If the attack is not centered on the body, it may also be possible to roll the punch or kick off the body by a quick rotation. In any case, the rotation of the hips and body will add power to the blocking technique. A third component of any defensive maneuver involves shifting the body. This is usually done to the rear or at an angle. The body shift places greater distance between the defender and attacker. It is possible to thwart an opponent's attack by using any one of the three components. For instance, shifting the body out of range will afford adequate protection and may be sufficient; however, it is best to use all three components together whenever possible. This will give you the best chance of defending yourself.

Blocks Using the Legs

The legs may also be used to block a kicking attack. Basically, the knee is raised high in the path of the oncoming kick, and the kick is absorbed by the muscles of the upper leg. In other blocks, such as *nami-ashi*, the foot may be snapped upward and inward from the floor, in order to strike the attacker's leg and deflect the

Figure 10-7: Blocking a front kick using the upper leg

kick. Still another method of using the legs to block involves thrusting the side edge of the foot against the opponent's ankle as he begins his kick.

The word *uke* is the Japanese term used to describe "blocks." The main blocks are *age-uke*, which means "rising block"; *gedan-barai*, which means "downward block"; *chudan-ude-uke*, which means "outside block"; *uchi-uke*, which means "inside forearm block"; *shuto-uke*, which means "knife-hand block"; and *mawashi-kake-uke*, which means "circular hooking block."

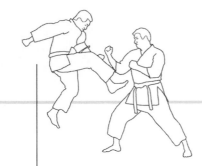

hand
techniques

KARATE, as a fighting art, is much different from Western boxing. The sport of boxing permits punches only with the forward part of the fist, which is covered by a padded glove. Karate practitioners use the bare fist, but use all parts of it, as well as a number of techniques with the open hand. In addition to the fore-fist, the back of the fist and the bottom are also used. In a similar manner, they use various parts

Figure 11-1: Training the reverse punch on the makiwara

of the open hand as well, including the side edges of the hand, the heel of the palm, and the fingertips. Blocking techniques also employ other parts of the hand, such as the back, side edge, or back of the bent wrist. Since there is no padding used on the hand, it must be strengthened and toughened so that it will not be damaged upon impact with the opponent. In traditional karate training, the hand is conditioned for striking when one practices the various attacking techniques against the makiwara, or striking post. This training device is unique to karate and has been used since it developed on Okinawa. One may practice any of the strikes against the makiwara, but the straight punch is the most commonly practiced. The heavy bag and other targets are also useful.

Hand Positions

Fore-Fist

Punching with the fore-fist, *seiken*, is the most common type of karate hand technique. The striking surface is the front of the first two knuckles. In order to use this effectively, your hand must be rolled into a tight ball and held straight on the wrist. Constant practice against the makiwara will strengthen the fist, wrist, and forearm, making the fist into a strong weapon. Repetitious push-ups on the first two knuckles will condition them for impact as well. Karate experts sometimes use a straight punch to break boards or other objects during demonstrations. One must take care to use only the first two knuckles. If you hold your fist straight out from your wrist, you can easily see that the first two knuckles are in line with the hand and arm. The outside two knuckles are smaller and do not have as much support. Striking an object with the outside knuckles may cause them to break. Numerous punching techniques utilize the fore-fist. Among them are the straight punch, lunge punch, reverse punch, roundhouse punch, jab, hook punch, scissors punch, U-punch, parallel punch, vertical-fist punch, close punch, and rising punch.

The most common hand positions are *seiken*, which means "fore-fist"; *uraken*, which means "back-fist"; *kentsui*, which means "bottom-fist" or "hammer-fist"; *shuto*, which means "knife-hand"; *ippon-ken*, which means "one-knuckle fist"; *hiraken*, which means "fore-knuckle fist"; *haito*, which means "ridge-hand"; *ippon-nukite*, which means "one-finger spear-hand"; *nihon-nukite*, which means "two-finger spear-hand"; *yonhon-nukite*, which means "four-finger spear-hand"; and *teisho*, which means "palm-heel."

Back-Fist

The back-fist, *uraken*, is another commonly used part of the hand. It is generally used in the performance of back-fist strikes to the face and head. In this case, the top of the first two knuckles is the striking area. As with the fore-fist, the fist must be clenched tightly in order to prevent injury to the hand.

Bottom-Fist

The bottom of the fist is sometimes referred to as the fist-hammer, or *kentsui*. It is frequently employed in blocking techniques, particularly the downward block. It is also used in many striking techniques to the side and in a downward motion.

Knife-Hand

The knife-hand, or *shuto*, is used in the performance of what people generally refer to as the "karate chop." The striking part of the hand is the outside edge, between the base of the little finger and the heel of the hand. To prevent injury, the hand must be held straight with the fingers tightly together and the thumb cocked back. Since the edge of the hand has a small surface area, strikes to the side of the neck or other soft parts of the body are particularly effective. The knife edge is also used in several blocking techniques, such as the knife-hand block, shuto-uke, the rising knife-hand block, age-shuto-uke, and the vertical knife-hand block, *tate-shuto-uke*.

One-Knuckle Fist

The one-knuckle fist, *ippon-ken*, is used to attack small targets, such as the point below the nose or the solar plexus. In this hand position, the striking surface is the point of the first knuckle of the hand, which protrudes from the fist. To reinforce the first finger, the thumb is pressed against its side. A variation of this is the middle-finger knuckle fist, *nakadaka-ippon-ken*, in which the knuckle of the middle finger is extended from the fist and used as the striking point.

Fore-Knuckle Fist

The fore-knuckle fist, *hiraken*, uses the point of the four knuckles as the striking surface. The hand is held straight on the wrist and open, with the knuckles of all four fingers extended forward. To do this, the fingers are bent back sharply at the first joint, and the thumb is tensed on the side of the hand. This fist is used against small targets such as the point under the nose or the larynx.

Ridge-Hand

The ridge-hand, *haito*, is used primarily against soft targets, such as the side of the neck or the ribs. It is formed in much the same way as the knife-hand, but the thumb must be turned inside to the palm area so that it is not damaged during the strike. The striking surface of the hand is the edge on the thumb side, between the base of the index finger and the heel of the hand.

Spear-Hand

There are three varieties of spear-hands. They are the one-finger spear-hand, *ippon-nukite*; the two-finger spear-hand, *nihon-nukite*; and the four-finger spear-hand, *yonhon-nukite*. These are primarily used to attack soft targets such as the eyes or the solar plexus. The four-finger variation is the most commonly seen, as it is included in many kata. The four-finger spear-hand is formed by holding the open hand straight and tensed. The middle finger is bent slightly so that the tips of the three fingers are even. The one- and two-finger spear-hands are formed the same way, with the other fingers bent back into the palm. The thumb is bent and tensed on the side of the hand.

Palm-Heel

The palm-heel, *teisho*, is a strong technique frequently used in blocking or in attacking the opponent's chin. It is formed by bending the open hand backward at an angle close to ninety degrees. The striking surface is the heel of the hand, just next to the wrist.

Hand Parts Used in Various Hand Techniques

Type of Technique	Part of Hand Used
Straight thrusts	Fore-fist, 1-, 2-, 4-finger spear-hand, fore-knuckle, one-knuckle, middle-knuckle, palm-heel, ox-jaw hand, elbow
Strikes	Knife-hand, ridge-hand, palm-heel, bottom-fist, back-hand, bear-hand, bent wrist, eagle-hand, chicken-head wrist, elbow

Other Hand Positions

Many other hand positions are also used to attack the opponent or block his technique. They are not frequently used but do have certain applications in special situations. They are the ox-jaw hand, *seiryuto*; the bear-hand, *kumade*; the chicken-head wrist, *keito*; and the eagle-hand, *washide*. Many of these techniques are frequently seen in advanced kata.

Thrusts and Strikes

Let's begin by understanding the difference between a thrust and a strike. Simply put, in a thrust, the attacking part of the hand or foot travels to the target in a straight line from its beginning to ending position. In performing a strike, the attacking part of the hand or foot travels in a circular movement to the target. We will concern ourselves here with hand techniques and will cover kicking techniques later.

Thrusts and strikes are not limited to any particular part of the hand. Thrusts may be performed using the fore-fist, palm-heel, one-knuckle fist, or any of the spear-hand techniques. Normally, the beginning position for the hand is palm up, just above the hip. It is then thrust in a straight line to the target. This may be done with the body in a stationary position or while it is moving. The most common of the thrusting techniques is the straight punch, *choku-zuki*, which is usually done as a lunge punch, *oi-zuki*, or a reverse punch, *gyaku-zuki*.

Hand Strikes

Lunge Punch

To perform the right lunge punch to the midsection, begin in the front stance with your left leg forward, your right hand at your right hip, and your left hand in the downward block position. Begin movement forward by flexing your rear ankle and driving your body forward. Make sure that your body is in an upright position and that your hips are not thrust to the rear as you

Figure 11-2: Lunge punch

move. As your right foot passes the left and nearly finishes the step, punch with your right hand and withdraw the left to your side. If you have done the lunge punch correctly, the movement of both your hand and foot should stop at the same time.

Figure 11-3: Reverse punch

Reverse Punch

Another very common type of punch is the reverse punch, or gyaku-zuki. As you stand facing your opponent, it is normal to block with the hand closer to him and counterattack with the hand that is farther away. Since the technique is most frequently used in this defensive manner, it is sometimes referred to as the counterpunch. To execute a reverse punch, begin in the front stance with your left leg forward, your right hand on your hip, and your left hand in the downward block position. Your body is in a side-facing position, with your hips turned to the side. Rotate your hips forward as you begin the punch, and then thrust your right fist to the target. Simultaneously withdraw your left hand to your left side. Exhale as you punch. The description of hip rotation here may give a false impression. In order to generate more power in the punch, your hips should be snapped around, not simply rotated.

Back-Fist Strike

As noted above, strikes follow a circular path to the target. The most common of these is the back-fist strike, uraken, which may be performed to the front or side. Another common strike is the knife-hand

Figure 11-4: Back-fist strike

Those main hand strikes are *choku-zuki*, which means "straight punch"; *oi-zuki*, which means "lunge-punch"; *gyaku-zuki*, which means "reverse punch"; *uraken*, which means "back-fist strike"; and *shuto-uchi*, which means "knife-hand strike."

strike, or *shuto-uchi*. Both of these techniques have many variations and may be aimed at targets to the front, side, or rear.

To perform a basic back-fist strike, bring your right fist to a position just in front of your left shoulder. The palm is down. Using your elbow as a pivot point, snap your fist forward to the target. As the fist approaches the target, it is rotated ninety degrees, so that the back of the first two knuckles will be the striking surface. The fist is not held at the ending point of the strike, but rather snapped back to the starting position. Back-fist strikes like this travel to the target in a path parallel to the ground. They may also take an upward, downward, or angular path.

Knife-Hand Strike

The knife-hand strike may be delivered from the outside inward, or from the inside outward. It may also be aimed at an opponent whose body position has placed him below you. In that case, it would travel a downward path.

Figure 11-5: Knife-hand strike

To perform the outside knife-hand strike, bring your left hand to the front of your body and your right knife-hand high to the side of your head. Snap the knife-hand toward the target in a circular movement. As you are about to hit the target, snap your wrist so that your palm is up. Simultaneously withdraw your left hand to your side. This may also be done from the outside inward by placing the palm of the striking hand against the opposite side of your head and then swinging it forward to the target. In the finished position, the palm is held downward.

Elbow Strikes

The elbow is also used as a powerful attacking surface. It may travel to the target as a thrust or a strike, depending on the beginning position and the location of the target. Thrusts are usually done to the rear, side, and downward, while strikes are upward or to the front, using a circular movement. These elbow thrusts and strikes are short-range techniques.

Figure 11-6: Rising elbow-strike

Rising Elbow-Strike

To perform the right rising elbow-strike, *age-empi-uchi*, begin with your right fist in the ready position just above your right hip, palm upward. Keeping your fist close to your chest, swing the point of your elbow upward toward the center of your body. Rotate your hips as you do the technique. The target is your opponent's chin. As you swing your elbow upward, sharply withdraw your other hand to your side.

Roundhouse Elbow-Strike

To perform the right roundhouse elbow-strike, *mawashi-empi-uchi*, begin with your left hand in front of your body and your right fist at the ready position above your right hip. Keeping your right fist close to your chest, rotate the point of your right elbow in a circular movement to the front, stopping at about the middle of your body. During this movement, the forearm is kept parallel to the ground. Your opposite hand is simultaneously withdrawn to your side.

The main elbow strikes are *age-empi-uchi*, which means "rising elbow-strike"; *mawashi-empi-uchi*, which means "roundhouse elbow-strike"; *yoko-empi-uchi*, which means "side elbow-thrust"; *otoshi-empi-uchi*, which means "downward elbow-thrust"; and *ushiro-empi-uchi*, which means "rear elbow-thrust."

Figure 11-7: Side elbow-thrust

Side Elbow-Thrust

To perform the left side elbow-thrust, *yoko-empi-uchi*, bring your left hand across your body to the right, with your forearm parallel to the ground and your palm downward. Thrust the point of your elbow to the left side. As you do this, bring your right hand sharply to your right side, palm up, and exhale.

Downward Elbow-Thrust

To perform the downward elbow-thrust, *otoshi-empi-uchi*, bring your right arm straight overhead, with your palm facing forward. In a sharp movement, bring your elbow downward and turn your wrist so that your palm faces inward toward your face. As with other techniques, exhale and bring your left fist to the ready position at your left hip.

Rear Elbow-Thrust

The rear elbow thrust, *ushiro-empi-uchi*, basically follows the same motion as withdrawing your arm to your side when punching.

leg techniques

KICKING TECHNIQUES are numerous and may be delivered in a wide variety of ways. They may be aimed at opponents to the front, side, or rear. Some of the kicks are thrust toward the opponent in much the same way that the hand may be thrust forward, and others follow a circular path to the target. The circular kicks are not referred to as strikes, but rather as snap-kicks. Accordingly, kicking techniques are of two types: snap-kicks and thrust-kicks. Generally speaking, snap-kicks are used for targets that are close in, while thrust-kicks are aimed at targets that are at a slightly greater distance. In all kicking techniques, the supporting foot must be flat on the floor and the supporting knee flexed for good strength and balance. The kicking foot is always withdrawn quickly and returned to the floor as soon as possible. Standing on one leg makes the kicker highly vulnerable to attack.

Parts of the Foot Used in Kicking Techniques

Kicking Technique	Part of the Foot Used
Front kick	Ball of foot, instep, tips of toes
Side kick	Side edge of foot
Back kick	Heel, sole of foot
Roundhouse kick	Ball of foot, instep
Knee kicks	Point of knee

Parts of the Foot Used in Kicks

Various parts of the foot are used in the execution of kicks. Which part to use is determined not only by the type of kick, but also by the target. Hard targets, such as the side of the head, need strong foot parts, whereas softer targets may be attacked using parts of the foot that are not that strong. The ball of the foot (*koshi*) and the heel (*kakato*) are the strongest. The side edge (*sokuto*), the instep (*haisoku*), and the tips of the toes (*tsumasaki*) are not as strong and are primarily used against softer targets.

Figure 12-1: Front snap-kick

Front Kicks

Front Snap-Kick

The front snap-kick, *mae-geri-keage*, is the most commonly used kick in karate. It is usually the first kick that one learns and is probably the last kick one is able to perform at an advanced age. This is because the front kick most closely follows the natural movement of the body when we are walking. The ball of the foot is the usual striking surface for this kick, but it may also be performed with the instep or pointed toes against soft targets such as the groin.

To perform a basic front snap-kick, stand in the left front stance with your hips facing to the side. Rotate your hips forward and raise your knee high to the front. As your knee approaches its highest point, snap the ball of your foot forward to the target and quickly snap it back. Do not stand on one leg for long, as this is a vulnerable position. As with all kicks, place the kicking foot back on the ground as soon as possible, in order to be prepared for the next technique, be it offensive or defensive.

Front Thrust-Kick

The front thrust-kick, *mae-geri-kekomi*, begins in the same manner as the front snap-kick, with the knee raised high to the front. As your knee reaches its

Figure 12-2: Front thrust-kick

maximum height, thrust the ball of your foot in a straight line to the target. Rotate your hips toward the target in order to add to the power of the kick. The foot may also be bent upward and the heel used as the striking surface. This is particularly useful for low targets such as a knee, or against an opponent who has fallen to the ground.

There are two types of kicks: the snap-kick for close targets and the thrust-kick for targets a little farther away.

Figure 12-3: Side snap-kick

Side Kicks

Side Snap-Kick

The side snap-kick, *yoko-geri-keage*, is a close-range technique used against an opponent positioned to one's side. To perform the basic side snap-kick, bring your knee high to the side, with the kicking foot placed near your supporting knee. In this position, your foot is held straight with your toes bent upward so that the side edge of your foot may be used as the striking surface. The side edge of your foot is then snapped outward to the target and immediately returned to your knee area and then to the floor. This is done in one smooth motion; do not pause with one foot against your knee. As you snap your foot outward, rotate your hips in the direction of the kick, to add to the force.

Figure 12-4: Side thrust-kick

Side Thrust-Kick

The side thrust-kick, *yoko-keri-kekomi*, is a longer-range kick than the side snap-kick. Since the foot travels a greater distance to the target and the hips have a major role, it is a more powerful kick. To execute the side thrust-kick, raise your knee high to the front of your body, with your foot next to your supporting knee. Thrust the side edge of your foot to the target, using a powerful rotation of your hips to propel your foot outward. As your foot strikes the target, instantaneously lock your knee and then, as the kick is completed, quickly withdraw your foot to the knee and then back to the floor.

The main side kicks are *yoko-geri-keage*, which means "side snap kick," and *yoko-keri-kekomi*, which means "side thrust-kick."

Back Kicks

There are actually several varieties of back kick: the back thrust-kick *(ushiro-geri-kekomi)*, the back snap-kick *(ushiro-geri-keage)*, and the back roundhouse kick *(mawashi-ushiro-geri)*.

Back Thrust-Kick

To perform the back thrust-kick, raise your right knee to the front of your body, with your foot near the supporting knee. As you do this, look over your right shoulder. As you thrust the heel of your kicking foot rearward, lean forward so that you may perform the kick easily. The kick should be aimed to the center line of your body. Quickly withdraw your kicking foot to your knee and then to the floor.

Back Snap-Kick

To perform the back snap-kick, simply bring your foot upward from the floor to the rear of your body. This is usually used against the opponent's groin, and the kicker may use the sole of the foot or the heel as the striking surface.

Figure 12-5: Back thrust-kick

Back Roundhouse Kick

The back roundhouse kick begins with the kicker facing his opponent, usually in a front stance. Stand in the left front stance. With a quick rotation of your hips and body in a clockwise direction, bring your right foot forward and swing your leg upward toward the target. The striking surface is your heel. This kick is frequently used as a follow-up in combination with a side thrust-kick or roundhouse kick, as the body is already in the middle of a rotation.

Roundhouse Kick

The roundhouse kick, *mawashi-geri*, is used against an opponent who is at the front or side, and it may be directed at any part of his body, from the knee to the head. The normal striking surface is the ball of the foot; however, the instep is sometimes used against soft targets such as the side of the neck or the ribs.

Begin the roundhouse kick in the left front stance. Raise your right knee high to the side with your foot cocked behind your body. Simultaneously pivot

Figure 12-6: Roundhouse kick

on your supporting foot, rotate your hips in a counterclockwise motion, and snap your right foot toward the target. Since this is a snapping kick, the foot is snapped back to the ready position. As with all kicks, this may be performed against most targets, using either the front or rear leg. Variations of this kick are many, and in some cases the knee is not brought high to the side, but more toward the target.

Figure 12-7: Crescent kick

Crescent Kick

The crescent kick, *mikazuki-geri*, is used as either an attack or a block. The striking surface for this kick is the sole of the foot. To practice the crescent kick, stand in the straddle stance and extend your left open hand to the left side of your body. Keep your arm straight and your thumb up; it will serve as a target for your kick. Pivot on your left foot and swing your right foot high to the front of your body and around to the side as you strike your palm with the sole of your right foot. As you place your right foot on the ground, assume the straddle stance and strike your left palm with your right elbow in a roundhouse elbow-strike. This is a common practice method. The kick may also be used as a block, with the sole of the foot used against an attacker's arm or wrist.

The main back kicks are *ushiro-geri-kekomi*, which means "back thrust-kick"; *ushiro-geri-keage*, which means "back snap-kick"; and *mawashi-ushiro-geri*, which means "back roundhouse kick."

Jumping Kicks

Front Jump-Kick

The front jump-kick, *mae-tobi-geri*, may be performed using one, two, or three kicks. Normally, it is used as a double kick, with the first kick distracting the opponent and setting him up for the second kick. Since the kicker must give

Figure 12-8: Front jump-kick

up his balanced position on the floor, this type of kick is dangerous to use and requires great agility and speed.

To practice the mae-tobi-geri using two kicks, *nidan-geri*, stand in the left front stance. Shift the weight of your body forward and push off the ground with your left foot. As you do this, raise your right knee high and execute a front snap-kick as you are leaving the ground. As you are in the air, withdraw your right foot, raise your left knee high, and execute a second kick. Withdraw your kicking foot quickly and land in the front stance with your left leg forward.

The word geri is the Japanese term used to describe "kicks." The main front kicks are *mae-geri-keage*, which means "front snap-kick," and *mae geri-kekomi*, which means "front thrust-kick."

Figure 12-9: Side jump-kick

Figure 12-10: Front knee-kick

Side Jump-Kick

Side kicks may also be performed while jumping. To perform the side jump-kick, *yoko- tobi-geri*, stand in the left front stance. Step forward with your right foot, flexing your knee sharply. Spring off the ground, raising your left knee high. While in the air, thrust the side edge of your left foot to the target. As you do this, snap your right foot upward to cover your groin area against a counterkick. Withdraw your feet quickly and land in the front stance.

Other variations of jumping kicks include jumping roundhouse kicks (*tobi-mawashi-geri*) and jumping back-kicks, either thrusting (*tobi-ushiro-geri-kekomi*) or spinning (*tobi-ushiro-mawashi-geri*).

Knees

Knees may also be used as weapons against your opponent. Use of the knee is limited to short-range targets. When an opponent attempts to grab you, he will be at a close range, and a kick may not be possible. Use of the knee in an upward or roundhouse manner may be indicated. It is not uncommon to begin a kick and then have the opponent charge into you to block it. Under these circumstances, the front kick may be rapidly changed into a knee kick.

*O*ther important karate kicks include *mawashi-geri*, which means "roundhouse kick"; *mikazuki-geri*, which means "crescent kick"; *mae-tobi-geri*, which means "front jump-kick"; and *yoko-tobi-geri*, which means "side jump-kick."

part 4
applying the basics

O NCE YOU HAVE LEARNED some of the basic techniques of karate, you have to understand how to apply them against a single opponent or multiple opponents. This can be accomplished in two ways. The first is through the practice of a variety of different sparring drills, using single or multiple opponents. The second is through the practice of kata, in which the opponents are imaginary. Let us begin with the practice of sparring drills.

chapter 13
sparring

TO DEVELOP KARATE SKILLS, one must learn and practice the basic movements and then learn to apply them against an opponent. The application of the techniques against an opponent is best learned by practicing a variety of drills, each of which is designed to help you master specific skills. Normally the first drill taught to students is the three-step sparring drill, or *sanbon-kumite*.

The first concept that we must understand is the idea of "no contact." As mentioned in chapter 7, most of the traditional karate schools practice what has come to be known as "no-contact" karate. This can be misleading. What it means is that punches, kicks, and strikes aimed at the opponent are pulled short of contacting the opponent's body. This is particularly necessary when the attack is aimed at the head. When the attack is aimed at the body, light contact is usually acceptable, although there will be some variation as to how

"Toughening" is necessary in your karate training because it teaches you to be familiar with the sensation of being blocked.

this is interpreted. In any case, the contact may be light, but not full force. Contact is perfectly acceptable when one practices blocking. You can expect to have some bruises on your arms and legs from being blocked by your opponent. Some schools permit the use of pads on the arms and legs to prevent bruising, but traditional schools usually do not. Why is this the case?

Suppose you are in a situation where you must use karate to defend yourself. You kick at your opponent, but his block strikes your shin and causes you great pain. If you are not used to this feeling, it may prevent you from staying

This chart indicates drills that emphasize particular skills, but it should be noted that one practices a variety of skills in any drill. These are some suggestions for improving skills through the practice of specific drills.

Sparring Drills and Learned Skills

Basic Skill to be Learned	Useful Drills
Correct application of blocks	One-step, three-step, five-step
Distancing	One-step, three-step, five-step, semifree-sparring
Timing	One-step, semifree-sparring
Linear movement	Three-step, five-step
Circular movement	One-step, semifree-sparing, free-sparring
Stance shifting	One-step, semifree-sparring

focused and pursuing the fight. Only by toughening the arms and legs will you be able to defend yourself. Some karate schools use specific exercises designed to toughen the arms and legs so that karate practitioners become accustomed to the feeling. After a while it will not be that bothersome and you will be able to withstand the block, since you will have toughened your body. Most schools of traditional karate will not allow the use of padding during training sessions, since they know that it will give students a false sense of security and that they will be unable to protect themselves in a confrontation.

Three-Step Sparring Drill

The first thing to note about all sparring drills is that they begin and end with both participants bowing to one another. This is a sign of mutual respect, and respect for others is an essential rule for karate practitioners. The purpose of the three-step sparring drill is to give the student practice in the basic elements of fighting, which include distancing, correct movement, blocking, attacking, and perception of attack. Of these, distancing is one of the most important

13-1a

Figure 13-1a–e: Three-step sparring drill

skills to be learned in this drill. Simply put, distancing (*maiai*) involves adjusting the space between yourself and your opponent so that you are in an ideal position to block and to deliver your attack. If you distance yourself too far from your opponent when you are on the attack, you will not be able to reach him, and your technique will easily be countered. If you are too close when you attack, you will not be able to develop maximum power in your kick or punch. On defense, if you are too far away, it will be impossible to deliver a counterattack to your opponent, and he may set you up for a kick. If you are too close, your opponent may overwhelm you, and you will be unable to deliver a strong counterattack.

13-1b

13-1c

To perform the three-step sparring drill, the opponents face each other about an arm's length apart. They bow to one another. The attacker steps back into the left front stance and performs a downward block with his left hand (Figure 13-1a). He then announces the target area, in this case *jodan*, or face level. The

defender waits in the ready position. As the attacker steps forward and performs a right lunge punch to the face, the defender steps back with his right foot and blocks with the left hand, using the rising block, age-uke (Figure 13-1b). The attacker steps forward twice more, both times attacking the face with left and then right lunge punches (Figures 13-1c and d). The defender uses the rising block to protect himself. After the third attack, the defender responds with a reverse punch to the midsection of the attacker (Figure 13-1e). As he does this, he kiais. Both sides then return to the *zanshin*, or ready, position. At this point, the roles are reversed and the drill goes in the other direction, with the defender becoming the attacker. The two sparring partners practice the drill with attacks to the face, midsection, and lower section, using the rising block (age-uke), the midsection block (ude-uke), and the downward block (gedan-barai).

Three-step sparring allows you to practice the basic elements of fighting: distancing, correct movement, blocking, attacking, and perception of attack.

It is important to note that both sides return to the zanshin position between sets. One of the skills to be mastered is the ability to move quickly from a normal everyday position to one of defense. Standing up between each drill gives constant practice in this movement. The drill ends with the opponents bowing to each other.

Many varieties of the three-step sparring drill are possible. The attacker may use three different levels of attack using the hands. He may also punch to the face, then to the midsection, and then execute a front kick. A series of three front kicks may also be used. Normally the defender will step back straight, but he may vary the practice and step at an angle as the last attack is launched toward him. Other variations of this sparring drill include five steps and seven steps.

The word *kumite* is the Japanese term used to describe sparring.

Let's see what is to be learned through the three-step sparring drill. The elements of fighting included here are (1) distancing; (2) timing; (3) proper use of blocking, attacking, and countering technique; and (4) perception of attack. All of these are important elements to master. Let's examine the distancing component. The opponent advances three times, and the defender has to adjust his distance so that he avoids the attack and also is in a position to counterattack. As the opponent takes the first step, the defender gets a sense of how far he can move. On the second step, his moving ability can be determined, and, on the third, the defender adjusts his step so that he is at the correct distance to initiate a strong counterattack. By training continually against a variety of opponents, tall and short, the karate practitioner can intuitively judge correct distance. The attacking side must also practice correct distancing, adopting the correct distance from his opponent prior to initiating the first attack. Through constant repetition of this drill, students will learn to adjust their distance automatically.

A second element to practice in this drill is correct timing. You must deflect the attacking punch or kick before it reaches the target, normally by blocking against the opponent's wrist or shin as he punches or kicks. Once the attacker has completed the punch or kick, it is too late—the defender will already have been hit. The attacking hand or foot must be deflected on its way to the target.

One must also practice the correct stance, block, and counterattack. Although the punch may be to the face area, the rising block, age-uke, may not be practical. If there is a significant difference in height between the two people doing the drill, it may be more practical to use one of the forearm blocks that are normally used for the midsection. When on the attack, make sure that your hips are straight, facing to the opponent, and that your posture is straight. Leaning forward, or in any position other than normal, will make it difficult to make the next move. On the defensive, use the side-facing position to block, and then rotate your hips forward to do the reverse punch, although any countering technique may be used.

Perception of attack is learned through countless repetitions. As your opponent initiates his kick or punch, his body will signal the beginning of the move. Once you have faced countless attacks, you will be able to detect these initial movements just as they begin. This will allow you to read your opponent, and you will be able to defend yourself or beat him to the punch. Normally you will practice such a drill against a variety of opponents, which will help you develop skill in adaptive movements.

One-Step Sparring

The one-step sparring drill is usually called *ippon-kumite*, but is also known as *kihon-kumite*, or basic sparring. Although this drill seems to be simpler than the three-step drill, it is actually more advanced. The emphasis here is on making an appropriate block and an instantaneous counterattack so that the opponent cannot follow up his initial attack with a second one. In the three-step drill, the defender had three chances to gauge his opponent's attack and prepare to distance himself correctly for it. In the one-step drill, there is only one chance, and if the defender does not adjust automatically, he may fail to block the attack or may not be in a correct position to counterattack. As in the three-step drill, there is only one chance to counterattack and only one chance for the attacker to score with his technique. This emphasis on one strong technique is a standard practice in most karate styles. The idea of only one chance reflects actual combat conditions. In a real fight, you may have only one chance to finish your opponent, since there may be other attackers about to come at you.

To perform the one-step drill, the opponents face each other and bow. The attacking side steps back with his right foot into the front stance, simultaneously blocking downward with his left hand (Figure 13-2a). After announcing the target area, *chudan* (midsection), he then steps forward and executes a right lunge punch to his opponent's midsection. His opponent steps back with his right foot and blocks with a left outside forearm block (Figure 13-2b). He then counterattacks with a right reverse punch to his opponent's solar plexus

13-2a

13-2b

13-2c

Figure 13-2a–c: One-step sparring drill

(Figure 13-2c). Similarly, the drill is repeated on the opposite side, in order to develop techniques on both sides of the body. Attacks to other areas such as the face or lower body may be used, and there is no limit to the type of counterattacking technique that may be performed. Kicks may also be used by the attacker or the defender.

One-Step Two-Attack Sparring

Another drill, still more advanced, requires that the defender thwart two attacks. In this drill, the attacker assumes the ready position for the attack, using the front stance as in the beginning of the one-step drill. After announcing the target areas, jodan and chudan (face and midsection), he then steps forward and attacks the defender with a lunge punch to the face and then immediately with a counterpunch to the midsection. The defender must block both attacks and then counter. Normally this is done with the same blocking hand. The first attack may be blocked with the rising block, and the midsection attack with a downward block or forearm block. The counterattack must be immediate.

Two-Step Two-Attack Drill

This drill has the attacker step twice and perform two different attacks. It requires that the defender block two attacks and then counterattack. After bowing, the two opponents face one another in the front stance. The attacker has his left foot forward, and the defender his right. The attacker announces the target area, jodan, and then steps forward, executing a right lunge punch to the face. The defender steps back with his right foot and executes a left rising block. The attacker then executes a left front snap-kick to the defender's midsection. The defender steps back with his left foot at a forty-five degree angle to the left, executing a downward block. He then counters with a reverse punch.

Target areas are referred to as *jodan*, which means "face," *chudan*, which means "midsection," and *gedan*, which means "lower section."

The opponents resume the ready position and reverse their roles. This drill may be practiced in a variety of ways, with different attacks and defensive movements being used.

Direction-Reversing Drills

One of the important skills that one must develop is the ability to rapidly shift from backward to forward movement. This is particularly useful when the opponent attacks using only a single technique and then backs off. The ability to follow instantly will allow one to score on the opponent.

The direction-reversing drill begins with a bow, and then the attacking side steps back into the front stance and performs the downward block. After announcing the target area, jodan, he steps forward and attacks his opponent with a lunge punch to the face. The defender steps back and blocks, and then steps forward and executes a lunge punch to the midsection of the attacker, who is now on the defense. The former attacker steps back, performing a midsection block and using a reverse punch to finish the drill.

Numerous variations of this drill are possible, with punches to the head or midsection used as well as front kicks. The last defensive movement is frequently at an angle, rather than straight back. The emphasis in this drill is on the direction-reversing movement. It is important to maintain good body position and balance as well as perform strong blocks and attacks.

Multiple-Attacker Drills

Karate has been designed to provide protection against one or more assailants. Therefore, it is necessary to practice against more than one opponent. This may be done in a variety of ways, using two, three, or as many as a dozen training partners to attack a single defender. After thwarting each attack, the defender must look at the next attacker prior to performing his block and countering techniques.

Two-Man Drills

In this drill, the defender is faced with two attackers, one in front and one in back. They are both positioned about one step from the defender. After bowing, the attackers step back into the left front stance and perform the downward block. The attacker in front steps forward and executes a right lunge punch to the face. The defender steps back in the right front stance and blocks the punch using a rising block. He then counterattacks with a reverse punch. As soon as the punch is completed, the second attacker steps forward and also punches to the defender's head, using a right lunge punch. The defender swings his rear foot to the right and turns to face his new attacker in the front stance. He thwarts the attack using a high inside forearm block with his right arm, and then executes a reverse punch to the attacker's midsection.

This drill may be varied in any number of ways, with the attackers using punches to the midsection, kicks, or other attacking techniques. The defender may use any block, punch, or kick combination. An alternate to the drill may position the attackers with one on each side of the defender. If there is only one training partner, the first of the attackers may be imaginary, and the defender can execute a block and punch and then turn to meet the new attack.

Four-Man Drills

Another drill uses four opponents. They are positioned in front, behind, and to the sides of the defender. They attack one at a time, each using the same technique. The defender faces each one in turn, blocking and countering their attacks. This type of drill gives excellent practice in body shifting and distancing, as constant adjustment of one's position is necessary. As with the two-man drill, any number of the opponents may be imaginary if the number of class members training during the session is not sufficient.

Circle Drill

In this drill the number of attackers may vary according to the number of students training. The attackers form a circle around the defender, who is in the middle. After bowing, the attackers assume the ready position for the attack—that is, the downward block in the front stance. One at a time, they each attack the defender with a lunge punch to the head. He must shift and meet each attack in turn, making sure that he blocks the attack and counters with a strong technique. In these multiple-attack drills, the principle of one strong counterattack is obvious. As soon as one attacker has been stopped, the next attacks. There is no second chance for a technique if the defender misses. The next attacker is soon upon him.

The attackers may use a variety of techniques, as may the defender. However, these drills are all prearranged, so the attackers must indicate their target. The drill may proceed with the attackers following one another in a clockwise movement until all have attacked, and then they may reverse direction and attack following a counterclockwise sequence. As each attacker finishes his attack and is countered, he steps back to the ready position so that the next attacker may begin his movement. Still another variation of this drill has each of the attackers assigned a number. The instructor calls out numbers at random, and the attackers then launch their techniques. In this manner, the defender must constantly be ready to move in any position. This variation is more useful for intermediate and advanced practitioners.

Double-Line Drill

The attackers form two lines, spaced about four feet apart. They assume the downward block position in the front stance. The defender then begins to walk between the two lines from beginning to end. Each of the attackers will take a turn attacking the defender, alternating from one side to the next. The defender is free to use any block-and-counter combination. Attacks may be prearranged or at random, depending on the experience of the students.

Continuous-Attacker Drill

This drill makes it necessary for the defender to use blocking techniques exclusively, as it is not possible to move the body backward or to the side. The defender stands in the front stance with his rear foot against the wall. In this position, it is impossible to move backward, and sideways movement is difficult. In front of him is a line of training partners, single file. Each, in turn, will attack using a prearranged attack, in this case a lunge punch to the face. The first opponent in the line assumes the front stance and then executes his attack. The defender blocks and counterpunches, and the attacker immediately steps away. As soon as he is out of the way, the next attacker executes a lunge punch to the face as well. This continues until all opponents in the line have attacked. If there are only a few members training, the line can start over again, and the attacks can continue until the defender has had sufficient practice. Alternates to the drill include punching attacks to the midsection and kicking techniques.

Semifree One-Point Sparring

This drill is known as *jiyu-ippon-kumite* and is more advanced than the rest. Although the attacking technique and target area are prearranged, it resembles free-fighting more than a drill. The exception is that the participants are only allowed one technique on the attack and one counterattack on defense. Once again, this reinforces the principle of having only one chance to finish the opponent.

The word *jiyu-kamae* is the Japanese term used to describe free-fighting stances.

After bowing, both sides assume their *jiyu-kamae*, or free-fighting stances. The attacker announces the target area and the technique to be used. The normal sequence of attacks would be lunge punches to the face and then the midsection. Kicks used in the attack would be the front snap-kick, side thrust-kick, and roundhouse kick, which would be targeted at the midsection and head. In order to help perfect the attacking technique, the rear leg is normally used for the kicking attacks. Both practitioners move around freely and, when the attacker senses that he is at the correct attacking distance and perceives an opening, he attacks. The defender is free to move in any direction and uses any block and counter technique. Having completed his technique, the attacker must maintain the ending position of his technique so that the defender may practice his counter. He is not permitted to block or step away to avoid the counterattack.

Varieties of this drill include announcing the target area and then attacking with any technique. It is also useful to have a third student act as a referee, noting which of the techniques in the exchange were effective and signifying which would effectively stop the opponent. Since this is a more advanced drill, it is suitable for intermediate and advanced students.

Line Drill

The line drill may be practiced in a variety of ways. The standard way is for two opponents to drill against one another. The offensive side practices continuous attacks, and the defensive side simply retreats before him, maintaining a stance suitable for counterattacking. The attacking side must concentrate on practicing consecutive techniques and combinations. The defensive side must retreat, but keep at an optimum distance for counterattacking. When an opening exists, he may counterpunch or kick, but must then retreat. This will give the defensive side good practice in maintaining balance and good hip position. Frequently this drill is practiced at half speed to allow the participants to execute movements correctly.

Slow-Motion Free-Style

In this drill, the participants move about and practice free-sparring, *jiyu-kumite*. However, they do not use any speed or power. They move as though there were a slow-motion camera on them. The emphasis in this drill is on smooth body movement. We have already noted how important it is to keep the body loose in order to increase speed of movement, but this is difficult to do when one is facing an opponent and sparring at full speed. Since there is no danger of being hit by a strong punch or kick, participants may relax and simply concentrate on building a variety of techniques. No points are scored here, and students are encouraged to remain at ease. They should concentrate on practicing different movements against their opponent.

If we make the drill into an actual full-speed match, then the two fighters will simply rely on their best technique in order to score a point. They will not experiment with new movements, since they will not want to take a chance. In that way, they will not develop diversified technique, but will only continue to practice their favorite techniques. This is a particularly difficult drill for intermediate students to learn, since they will have a hard time relaxing.

This practice may also be varied, with the speed stepped up to about three-quarters, but the emphasis again must remain on keeping loose and moving correctly.

One Side Attack—One Side Defend Drill

This is a variation on free-sparring. It is usually performed at about half to three-quarter speed, with the emphasis on keeping the body movement fluid. At the beginning of the match, one side is designated the attacker and one the defender. The attacker may use any technique against his opponent, and tries to score with a variety of techniques. The defender is allowed to move freely and counterattack whenever the opportunity presents itself. He may not go on the offensive, but must react to his opponent. This provides good practice in sideward and circular movement for the defender, who must short-circuit his opponent's attacks. After one side plays the attacker for a minute or so, they switch roles and the defender becomes the attacker.

Free-Style Fighting

The ability to practice free-style fighting, jiyu-kumite, is the result of intense training in the basic techniques. In a free-sparring match, both sides move about freely and execute techniques at full speed. They attempt to score against their opponents as many times as possible. Normally this is done under the watchful eye of the instructor so that injuries are kept to a minimum. It is not uncommon, however, for accidents to occur. Anyone who engages in free-style fighting will sooner or later get many bruises, some stitches, or a broken bone. Before you get scared off by this, it should be noted that in good schools with competent instructors, such mishaps are at a minimum. In schools where students have not been properly trained in the basics, or have been allowed to free-spar too soon, more injuries occur. We should also note here that karate training is no different from any other athletic activity. In karate, we may have a greater frequency of minor injuries such as cuts and broken fingers or toes, but other sports have them as well. A survey of any of the popular sports such as baseball, football, and basketball will demonstrate that certain injuries are common to each. When gauged against other athletics, karate is a relatively safe activity. That having been said, it is unreasonable for anyone to expect to participate in an athletic activity without running the risk of occasional injury. Karate, properly taught and supervised, causes fewer injuries than many other sports.

Developing a Strategy

Karate practitioners soon find that simply being able to kick, punch, and block does not guarantee success in a fight. One must also learn strategy. Normally this is a concern for black-belt ranks. Those below black belt are advised to concentrate on mastering basic movements and learning kata. After the first degree of black belt has been achieved, it is time to concentrate more on sparring.

 There are two parts to developing a fighting strategy: understanding your own body and understanding how to apply your techniques against an opponent.

There are two parts to developing a strategy. The first is understanding your own body, and the second is understanding how to apply your techniques against an opponent. Let's consider the first part. Everyone has strong and weak points. We must determine what our strong point is and use techniques that will work best for us. We all have our own body type, whether it is strong, flexible, stiff, or has any combination of attributes. A practitioner sixty years of age should realize that he may not effectively use a jumping side kick in a fight, but may successfully defend himself with a low kick to the shins or knees of his attacker. Learning what techniques are best for your body type is the first step in developing a strategy. If you have a limited ability to kick, then you may have to rely more on hand techniques to win. It goes without saying that

There are two types of fighting strategy: go no sen, which requires you to strike at the moment your opponent first begins his attack, and sen no sen, which requires you to attack as soon as you see an opening.

you must develop all of the techniques in the karate arsenal to their utmost; however, it may not be practical for you to use all of them in a fight. The first step in developing a strategy is understanding what will work for you, given your age, condition, and body type.

The second factor has to do with your opponent. You may have one who is much taller than you. Since the general principle of fighting is to hit the nearest available target, a kick to his head makes little sense. You will be able to score on him more effectively with a low attack. Similarly, if you tower over your opponent, his head will be closer to your hands, making his head the logical target.

In a practice match, you bow and then begin the fight. As soon as you begin to move, your opponent will either shift in, stand his ground, or shift away. Through continuous training in sparring, you will learn to read your opponent as quickly as possible. If you can see that his body shifting and movement are faster and better than yours, you cannot expect to beat him by outshifting him. Another strategy will work better. This is where experience comes into play. Suppose you find that he continually blocks all of your attempts to score with a kick. You may then fake a kick and attack using punching or striking techniques. Perhaps he continually crowds you, but weighs less than you do. This may be a good opportunity to seize his clothing, keep him close to you, and use elbows and knees. If he outweighs you, this would not be a good strategy, and it would be a better idea to operate at a distance, so that you cannot be overpowered and outwrestled.

Learning strategy is the result of a multitude of exercises. It begins when you learn basic techniques and practice basic sparring drills. Through them you learn how your own body moves, how others move, and what techniques seem most natural to you. In various drills you will see your own weak and strong points, as well as those of your opponents. Concentrate on your opponents as they advance toward you with punching and kicking attacks. Imagine what kind of counters you might use against them.

Watching others spar will also be most instructive. Observe how various fighters move. Note their strong and weak points, and try to exploit them when you have a match against them. Watch fighters in competition. You will see many advanced practitioners who demonstrate a variety of techniques. Here is where you can learn much and also make big mistakes. Note fighters with body types similar to yours and see what works for them. Watch also the fighters who use techniques that seem to get them in trouble, and try to analyze why this occurs.

It is not uncommon for beginners to watch successful competitors and try to copy their techniques. Usually the competitor who wins the kata competition regularly will have a favorite kata. Within a year or so, there will be any number of less experienced competitors doing the same kata in competition, wrongly thinking that the judges are voting for the kata, not for the performance of it. In the same way, the winner of the sparring competition will also demonstrate his *tokui-waza*, or favorite technique. Within a short period of time, the copycats will be at it again, and there will be any number of contestants mimicking his technique. This is a great mistake. You must develop your own karate that is suited to your body, not that of someone else. Many instructors will not perform sparring or kata in front of their students, since they realize that the students will try to copy them.

How do we determine the optimum time to attack the opponent? Or should we wait for him to attack, and then counter? These decisions are important ones and have led to the analysis of how strategy works. Basically there are two types of strategy, *go no sen* and *sen no sen*.

Go no sen requires that the opponent initiate his movement first. It is not necessary to allow him to complete the technique; it is not just block and counterattack. Rather it requires that you watch the opponent carefully and allow him to begin his movement. At the moment that he begins to initiate his attack, you strike before he completes it. This obviously requires great skill and extensive training. One may lure the opponent into an attack by giving him an opening, such as raising the lead arm so that the midsection is exposed. Having perceived an opening, the opponent may seize the opportunity to attack. However, you have read his movement and are in position to beat him to the punch.

Sen no sen is the strategy of attacking first, as soon as you see an opening. You do not allow the opponent to get focused or to plan his attack. Before he can get started, you charge in with a strong attack. This does not mean that you mindlessly charge into anyone's reverse punch; you must create an opening in one of two ways: actively or passively. Actively creating an opening implies that you do something to leave one of your opponent's vital points open. As an example, you might punch to the face. Your opponent will have to block upward, leaving the lower part of his body open to attack. Similarly, you might kick to the lower part of his body and follow up with a punch to the face. Passively creating an opening requires that you lure your opponent into thinking that you are vulnerable. Let's say that you lower your guard hand so that your head does not seem to be protected. Your opponent seizes this opportunity to punch to your face. Since this was your plan, you can easily block and counter with a strong technique. In both of the instances noted above, you are creating situations that will allow you to control your opponent and determine when he will attack, what technique he will use, and how he will move.

chapter 14
the kata

What Is a Kata?

A KATA may be considered to be two things. The first is an imaginary fight between the performer and several opponents. The second is a valuable training method that will allow the practitioner to train his or her body movement in a wide variety of ways.

As noted earlier, the kata is considered to be the backbone of karate. If we look at all of the kata practiced in the various Okinawan/Japanese systems, we can probably come up with about fifty. Some of them are relatively short and some quite long. Others have many basic moves, and in some the moves are

Figure 14-1: Karate class practicing *Heian Nidan* at the Kobukan Karate Club in Toms River, New Jersey

The word *kata* is the Japanese term used to describe formal exercises. There are two types of kata: Shorin and Shorei.

quite complex and acrobatic. Some are required for specific rank, while others are specialized forms that are practiced only by advanced black belts.

In our first discussion of the kata, we indicated that there were two types, Shorin and Shorei. The former emphasizes shifting and agility, while the latter emphasizes powerful movements. This idea can be misleading to students who think that kata of one type do not contain elements of the other. All kata may be divided into three levels of difficulty: beginner, intermediate, and advanced. The beginning and intermediate kata are practiced up to the first degree of black belt. Other intermediate and advanced kata are practiced by those who have already achieved black-belt rank.

How Is a Kata Useful?

Favorite Kata

Practicing particular kata will develop your strengths and improve your weaknesses. Normally one will practice a *tokui*, or favorite kata, only after one has achieved brown-belt rank. In most systems there will be a choice from several intermediate kata, and the student is supposed to choose one that suits his body style. If you have a strong and heavy body, then a kata that emphasizes strong technique will be your choice. Those who are lightweight and move easily should choose one that emphasizes speed and agility. It is a good idea to pick a second kata to work on as well. This should be an opposite type. So your favorite kata will emphasize your strengths, and your second kata will help to improve your weak points. For instance, if your stance is too high and you find that your opponent can easily drive you back or sweep you, it may be advisable to pick a kata that helps you develop a strong stance. The kata Sochin and *Chinte* both feature low, powerful stances, and these may help to develop your strength. Similarly, if your movement is stiff and awkward, you should pick a form such as *Empi* or *Kanku Sho*, both of which will require that you move rapidly and practice jumping and body shifting. This will help you to develop flexibility in movement.

Major Karate Systems and Their Kata

Shorin Ryu Systems	Fukyugata I, Fukyugata II, Pinan Shodan, Pinan Nidan, Pinan Sandan, Pinan Yondan, Pinan Godan, Naihanchi Shodan, Naihanchi Nidan, Naihanchi Sandan, Annaku, Wankan, Wanshu, Chinto, Gojushiho, Kusanku, Passai Sho, Passai Dai, Seisan, Rohai Jo, Rohai Chu, Rohai Ge, Hakutsuru
Goju Ryu	Sanchin, Tensho, Gekisai ichi, Gekisai ni, Kanchu, Saifa, Seiunchin, Seipai, Shisochin, Sanseru, Tensho, Kururunfa, Ryufa, Seisan, Suparinpe
Uechi Ryu	Sanchin, Seisan, Superunpe, Kanchiwa, Kanchin, Seryu, Kanshu, Sechin
Shotokan	Heian Shodan, Heian Nidan, Heian Sandan, Heian Yondan, Heian Godan, Tekki Shodan, Tekki Nidan, Tekki Sandan, Bassai Dai, Bassai Sho, Kanku Dai, Kanku Sho, Empi, Jitte, Jion, Hangetsu, Gankaku, Nijushiho, Gojushiho Sho, Gojushio Dai, Unsu, Wankan, Sochin, Chinte, Meikyo
Shito Ryu	Pinan Shodan, Pinan Nidan, Pinan Sandan, Pinan Yondan, Pinan Godan, Naihanchi Shodan, Naihanchi Nidan, Naihanchi Sandan, Jitte, Jion, Rohai, Bassai Dai, Bassai Sho, Kosokun Dai, Kosokun Sho, Shihi Kosokun, Chinto, Chintei, Wanshu, Gojushiho, Sanchin, Tensho, Seienchin, Seipai, Sanseiru, Saifa, Kururunfa, Suparinpei, Niseishi, Unsu, Sochin (Aragaki), Nipaipo, Jyuroku (Kenwa Mabuni), Seyriu (Kenwa Mabuni), Sihnpa, Sinsei (Miyagi), Matsumura Rohai, Matsumura Bassai, Tomari Bassai, Shisochin, Hakkaku, Pachu, Heiku, Paiku, Ahnan, Annanku, Seisan, Matsukaze, Ayoanagi
Wado Ryu	Pinan Shodan, Pinan Nidan, Pinan Sandan, Pinan Yondan, Pinan Godan, Naihanchi Shodan, Naihanchi Nidan, Naihanchi Sandan, Jitte, Jion, Kusanku, Chinto, Seisan, Passai, Niseishi

Kata Name Changes

Okinawan Name	Japanese Name
Pinan	Heian
Naihanchi	Tekki
Passai	Bassai
Kusanku or Koshokun	Kanku
Seishan	Hangetsu
Wanshu	Empi
Jitte	Jitte
Jion	Jion
Rohai	Meikyo
Chinto	Gankaku
Useshi	Gojushiho
Shokyo	Ji'in
Hakko	Sochin
Shoifu or Hito	Wankan
Niseishi	Nijushiho
Shoin	Chinte

The Value of Kata

To the uninitiated, the kata appears to be a dance that demonstrates various karate techniques. While this is true, there is much more going on when the kata is being performed. The karate practitioner begins and ends the kata with a bow, signifying his respect for his opponents. They are not visible, but they do exist in his own mind. In Western combative sports, such as boxing or wrestling, it is assumed that there is one opponent. This leads the wrestler or boxer to practice his movements in a particular way. In karate, there may be one opponent also, but since it is a true combat art, there may be several. Therefore, it is necessary to practice body movements that will allow the fighter to shift between these multiple attackers. If we examine the kata closely, we can see that there are peculiar turns and shifts that indicate that the performer is changing directions to face a new opponent after one has been eliminated.

One of the great benefits in practicing a variety of kata is that the practitioner will train his body movement for facing multiple assailants. Attackers from the rear and sides will be confronted in a well-balanced position, and the practitioner will be able to shift easily between them. Practicing kata is also a strenuous exercise that will benefit overall body conditioning and lead to mastery of all sorts of unusual body movements.

Different Styles and Their Kata

The kata listed in the chart on page 105 are representative of the various styles, but this is not an exhaustive list. In addition, kata that involve the use of weapons have not been included. These are part of *kobudo*, the practice of ancient weapons. Many of the karate systems include weapons in their training, particularly those that closely follow Okinawan tradition. Generally speaking, there is less practice of kobudo among the Japanese systems as compared to the Okinawan. In addition, high-ranked practitioners frequently study the kata of other styles, sometimes incorporating them into their training regimen. In some cases, if they are instructors, they will also teach the form to their students, even though it is not standard in the system they practice. In this manner, many of the Okinawan and Japanese karate styles have come to practice kata derived from both the Shorei and Shorin traditions. Keep in mind that many of the Okinawan masters who emigrated to Japan to teach karate brought with them kata of both types. Masters Kenwa Mabuni and Gichin Funakoshi, founders of Shito Ryu and Shotokan respectively, considered their karate to be a combination of both.

In the past, the kata was the main type of practice. Up until the 1920s in Japan, this was the primary kind of karate training.

It should be noted that although the kata practiced in various styles may have the same name, they will not automatically be the same. How can this be? Let's say that sixty years ago, five men practiced karate under a particular master, who taught all of them the kata *Bassai Dai*. Each would move differently, according to his body type. If each of the five opened his own school and taught ten people, there would doubtless be some variation, as each of the five new teachers would have his own interpretation of the kata and some modifications. As some of the kata are quite old, one can easily see how the various schools would practice them differently. Some instructors, being more flexible, might make the kicks higher, while others might simply keep the kicks aimed at a low target. Because of this, there are many variations of Bassai Dai practiced today.

It should also be noted that there are different readings of the kata characters between Okinawa and Japan. Thus the kata series known as *Pinan* on Okinawa is pronounced as *Heian* in Japan. In other cases, the kata had Chinese names and were renamed during the period of intense Japanese nationalism that existed prior to World War II. In this manner, *Kusanku* became known as *Kanku Dai* and *Naihanchi* as *Tekki*.

Following the Path—the Embusen

Kata always follow a predetermined line called the *embusen*. We may consider this to be a kind of floor plan. There are several common shapes for these embusen, and many follow an H or T pattern, while others are performed in a straight line. See Figure 14-2. Kata begin and end on the same spot. If your stepping is consistent and done correctly, the kata should end exactly where it began.

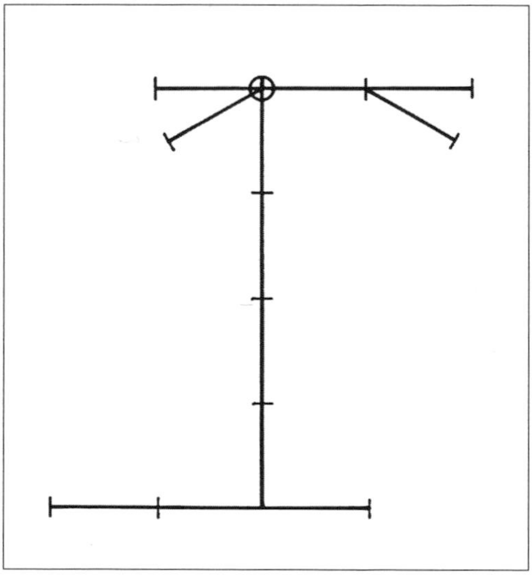

Figure 14-2: Embusen for Heian Shodan

Interpreting the Secrets in the Kata

The interpretation of kata movements was, and still is, considered essential to understanding the kata. Movements that seemingly have little connection to actual fighting will, upon closer examination, reveal methods of thwarting attacks and defeating the opponent. Over the years, many Okinawan karate masters have claimed that the Japanese have misinterpreted kata movements and have not fully understood them. The Japanese, by comparison, claim that they have developed karate further and that the old explanations were fine then but are not up to date. We don't have to take sides in this debate, but we should keep an open mind when it comes to kata interpretation.

The interpretation of kata is known as *bunkai*. Let's take a look at how this might work. To begin with, it is quite difficult to practice a kata correctly without understanding the meaning of the movements. In order to do this, it is necessary to practice the various kata movements against an opponent. Once this has been done, the practitioner has a real feeling for the movements. It is an easy matter for an instructor to see if his student understands the kata. If

The word *embusen* is the Japanese term used to describe the predetermined line followed when performing kata.

he does not, the movements will seem to have no purpose, as though the practitioner were simply waving his hands in the air and moving aimlessly about. When the student has practiced the various kata moves against an opponent, it will be quite obvious. After learning the correct sequence and rhythm for the kata, the next thing a student must learn is to apply the moves against an adversary. After having done so, the practitioner will actually begin to feel the presence of an opponent as he or she performs the kata.

The word *bunkai* is the Japanese term used to describe the interpretation of kata.

Since we will be practicing the kata *Heian Shodan* (Figure 14-2), let's take a look at a representative move. After bowing to his opponents, the practitioner makes the first move. He looks to the left and then steps in that direction, performing a left downward block in the left front stance. It is obvious to the observer that he is probably practicing a block against a kick to the midsection. That is certainly one interpretation; however, he might also be blocking a punch to the midsection, since the downward block might be used successfully against either. So we have two possible explanations for the move. But is that all? How can we apply this movement in other situations? Suppose that he was being attacked by an assailant who was trying to grab his legs and throw him to the ground? This might be a standard approach that a wrestler might take. Instead of blocking a kick, he might be using his blocking arm to strike his opponent's temple with the bottom of the fist. This would probably put the attacker out of action. Other uses for the movement can be determined as well. This is why students are told to study a kata, not just practice it. In the past, the study of a kata took several years, and after that time, many practitioners realized that they could still learn more from concentrating on it.

Heian Shodan

Heian Shodan is the first kata in the Shotokan system and in many other styles. Originally it was called *Pinan Nidan*; however, since *Pinan Shodan* had more complex moves, the names were switched and Pinan Nidan became known as Pinan or Heian Shodan in several styles. Others still keep the same designation, and thus this is the second kata in their system.

Figure 14-3a   Figure 14-3b   Figure 14-3c

Figure 14-4a

Figure 14-4b

Figure 14-5a

Figure 14-5b

Figure 14-6

Figure 14-7a

Figure 14-7b

Figure 14-8a

Figure 14-8b

Figure 14-9

Figure 14-10

Figure 14-11a

Figure 14-11b

Figure 14-12

Figure 14-13a

Figure 14-13b

Figure 14-14

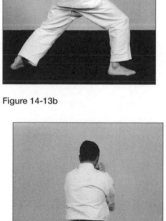

Figure 14-15a

Figure 14-15b

Figure 14-16

Figure 14-17

Figure 14-18

Figure 14-19a

Figure 14-19b

Figure 14-20a

Figure 14-20b

Figure 14-21a

Figure 14-21b

Figure 14-22a

Figure 14-22b

Figure 14-23

The Moves

There are twenty-one moves in Heian Shodan, beginning with the left downward block in the front stance and ending with the left knife-hand block in the back stance. The beginning and ending zanshin positions are not counted as movements. The number of figures used to illustrate the kata here is thirty-four, which includes the zanshin positions at the beginning and end.

Each kata begins and ends with a bow. Place your heels together in the informal attention stance, *musubi-dachi*, and bow. Assume the ready position, *shizentai*, by moving first your left and then your right foot to about one shoulders' width apart. The stance is *hachiji-dachi* (Figure 14-3a). Look to the left and then step out ninety degrees to the left in the front stance, *zenkutsu-dachi*. As you step, perform the downward block, *gedan-barai* (Figure 14-3b). Step forward in the right front stance and execute a lunge punch, *oi-tsuki*, to the midsection (Figure 14-3c). Look over your right shoulder and withdraw your right foot, turning 180 degrees to the right and executing a right downward block in the right front stance (Figure 14-4a, b). Quickly shift your front foot back about halfway to your left, *renoji-dachi*, and bring your right fist upward toward your body. Then shift back to the right front stance and strike the opponent with the right bottom-fist strike (Figure 14-5a, b). In the finished position, your fist will be about shoulder height. Step forward with your left foot into the left front stance and perform a left lunge punch to the midsection (Figure 14-6). Look to your left and then turn ninety degrees to the left in the front stance and perform a left downward block (Figure14-7a, b). In place, execute a left rising block with the knife-hand and then immediately step forward and perform a rising block, *age-uke*, with your right hand in the front stance (Figure 14-8a, b). Step forward twice more in the front stance, executing first a left and then a right rising block (Figures 14-9 and 14-10). After each of these rising blocks has been completed, open the blocking hand to the knife-hand position just prior to stepping forward to perform the next rising block. As you do the last rising block, *kiai*. Look to the right, bring the left foot up to the right, and then turn 270 degrees in a counterclockwise movement, ending in a left front stance and left downward block (Figure 14-11a, b). Step forward and perform a right lunge punch (Figure 14-12). Look over your right shoulder and turn 180 degrees to the right, performing a right downward block in the right front stance (Figure 14-13a, b). Step forward and perform a left lunge punch to the midsection (Figure 14-14). Look to your left. Step to the left ninety degrees and perform a left downward block in the front stance (Figure 14-15a, b). Step forward three times in the front stance, performing first a right, then a left, and then a right lunge punch to the midsection (Figures 14-16, 14-17, and 14-18). As you do the third punch, *kiai*. Look to the right, bring your left foot up to the right, and then turn 270 degrees in a counterclockwise movement ending in a left back stance, *kokutsu-dachi*, and performing a left knife-hand block, *shuto-uke* (Figure 14-19a, b). Step out forty-five degrees in a right back stance and perform a right knife-hand block (Figure 14-20a, b). Look to the right. Keeping your left foot in place, swing your right foot 135 degrees in a clockwise movement and execute a right knife-hand block in the right back stance (Figure 14-21a, b). Step out forty-five degrees to the left and execute a left knife-hand block in the left back stance (Figure 14-22a, b). This is the last action move of the kata, but it is not finished. Slowly withdraw your left foot and assume the *zanshin* position in *hachiji-dachi* (Figure 14-23). Bring your heels together and bow. Then assume the informal attention stance.

The Rhythm

One of the important aspects in the performance of a kata is the development of rhythm. Each kata is done to a specific one. This is designed to mimic the tempo of actual fighting. If you watch two combatants in any fighting art—wrestling, boxing, judo, or karate—it will be obvious that they do not perform at the same speed through the entire match. There are times when they move slowly to line up the opponent and then move quickly to execute a technique. They may also back off and pause momentarily before executing a technique. In other words, the rhythm of fighting is not consistent, it is broken. In the same way, the rhythm of a kata is broken. Generally speaking, movements that are directed at a specific attacker go together, with pauses between attackers. Let's look at the rhythm for Heian Shodan. After the bow and assumption of the ready position, the performer looks left, blocks, and then steps into the lunge punch. These two moves go together. Then there is a pause. He then turns 180 degrees to the rear, performs the downward block, shifts back and breaks his opponent's grip, and then does a left lunge punch. This opponent is finished, and there is a slight pause. He then turns left ninety degrees and blocks down. After a brief pause, he steps three times, performing rising blocks with a broken rhythm. The rhythm for the three is: one, then one-two. After the third rising block, there is again a slight pause before turning to meet the next attacker. Once again the downward block is quickly followed by a lunge punch. A slight pause follows, and then the performer turns 180 degrees to the rear and does another downward block and lunge punch combination. After pausing again, he turns ninety degrees to the left and executes a downward block. The series of three lunge punches follows the "one, then one-two" rhythm. After the third punch there is again a slight pause before the performer turns 270 degrees and performs a knife-hand block followed immediately by another. Then after another slight pause, the performer turns 135 degrees to the right and executes a right knife-hand block, and then immediately steps out forty-five degrees and does another. The action part of the kata has ended, and the performer holds his position for a few seconds and then returns to the zanshin, or starting position.

As noted above, each kata has a specific rhythm. Intermediate and advanced kata have numerous moves that are done in slow motion; many include tension in the movement. Although these seem to be easy moves, since they are slow they are actually more difficult to perform correctly. Great body control is needed to make the hand and foot stop at the same time so that the movement is coordinated just as it would be if it were performed at full speed.

The Timing

The kata has been completed. If you have performed Heian Shodan correctly, it has taken about forty seconds. Studies have determined that this is significantly faster than Heian Shodan was done earlier in the century. Films exist from the 1950s that demonstrate many of the kata, and if they are compared to films today, it is obvious that the timings have been changed. Records from the prewar era demonstrate that Master Funakoshi recommended about sixty seconds as the correct time to complete the form.

The difference in times probably reflects several things. First of all, we must consider the effect that karate competition has had on the art of karate. Once, individuals could train at a speed that seemed appropriate to them, but now they have to contend with the pressure of being viewed by many senior practitioners and many spectators. Such pressure has led to an increase in performance and speed. Second, today's karate athletes are probably better physical specimens than those who lived earlier in the century. This is evident by the breaking of records in all areas of athletics. It seems natural that karate practitioners today are capable of more efficient movement than those of the past.

Third, we must look at the effect of modernized training methods. In the past, a practitioner simply did kata as the main type of training. Today, a variety of training methods is in evidence, with much emphasis on training basic movement. It is natural that this should affect the ability of the practitioner to spar and do kata.

the training session

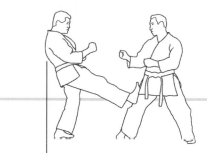

Behavior

N ORDER TO PARTICIPATE in a karate training session, it is necessary to be familiar with dojo etiquette. There are two primary factors that affect our behavior in the dojo: (1) the influence of Japanese/Okinawan culture and (2) the necessity for special behavior caused by the practice of a martial art.

Let's consider the influence of Japanese/Okinawan culture first. We are practicing a fighting art with roots in that area of the world. In order to fully appreciate the culture of karate and to derive the maximum benefit from it, it is necessary to experience some of the cultural aspects that accompany it. In Japanese culture, teachers are given great deference. In the dojo, the instructor is addressed as *Sensei*, which means teacher, although it is also acceptable to address an instructor as Mr. or Ms. Normally the instructor's name is given first and the title second. Thus the late karate master Masatoshi Nakayama, of the Japan Karate Association, would be referred to as Nakayama Sensei.

The second factor is the need for discipline, without which it would not be possible to learn this complex art. Karate techniques are dangerous, and in order for training to progress safely, the class must be well under the control of the instructor. This discipline, imposed from above, will assist the student in acquiring self-control, an important goal of training.

When the class is called to attention, you are to stand in zanshin, the ready position, until directed to perform movements. In zanshin, you are facing forward in one of the informal attention stances, usually hachiji-dachi or heikodachi. In this position, you are to imagine an opponent in front of you at all times. Wait for the instructor to give the signal to assume a fighting position, *kamae-te*. When the drill is completed, the instructor calls "*yame*," which means "stop." He then calls "*naore*." This is the signal for the students to relax after they have returned to the zanshin position to wait for the next set of drills to begin. If you need to fix your training uniform or wipe the sweat off your brow, turn to the rear and do it quickly. Once you face forward, you should be focused on an imaginary opponent in front of you. On occasion, the instructor will direct you to various parts of the training hall or tell you to sit down while others practice more advanced drills. All your movements to and from the practice area should be at double time. One does not slouch around or behave inattentively in the dojo.

The word *sensei* is the Japanese term for "teacher."

A student must learn how to bow in the correct manner, since this shows respect for others. To Westerners, this seems to be a bit unusual, since they do not normally bow. In Japan, however, it is the normal way for people to greet one another, and a way to show respect. Think of it as a handshake, which might be our closest equivalent. You will bow to the memory of the past masters when you enter the dojo and will bow to the instructor if he is present. When class begins, the instructor and class kneel and bow to one another. As you begin a sparring drill, you bow to your opponent in order to show respect.

Listen for these calls from your instructor: *yame*, which means "to stop," and *naore*, which means "to relax in the zanshin position."

You will do many sparring drills in which you will stand there after having performed your attack. Your opponent will use you for target practice but will not make contact. The bow also shows mutual trust, that we will train hard against one another but will not try to cause needless injuries to our training partners.

In classes where the ranks are mixed together, beginners may be asked to sit down while advanced drills or kata are being performed. The instructor may determine that you are not ready for that type of practice. Here is where additional knowledge of etiquette comes into play. When sitting during class, you must be in a position in which you can defend yourself. There are two types of acceptable sitting positions. The first is the standard kneeling position, just the same as the way in which you will bow in and out of class. The second is a seated position, with the legs drawn in and folded. In both of these positions, it is possible to move and defend oneself. Laying back with legs outstretched or leaning against the wall is sure to bring a reprimand from the instructor.

Belt Rank System

One of the most obvious features of karate culture is the belt rank system. To outsiders, the black-belt rank seems to epitomize the highest achievement in karate. However, serious karate practitioners know that there are fine distinctions between the ranks. Those who achieve the rank of first degree, or *Shodan*, are considered to be serious students who have achieved a good grasp of the fundamentals and now can begin to actually learn karate. Ranks of second and third degrees, *Nidan* and *Sandan*, indicate that good progress is being made along the path to karate mastery. It is said that almost anyone of average ability can achieve a Sandan rank if he trains long enough. A line is drawn at the level of the fourth and fifth degrees, *Yondan* and *Godan*. Practitioners who achieve these ranks are considered to have something special. Their talent in karate technique is far above that of their peers, and these ranks are considered to be high degrees. In many organizations, Godan is considered to be the highest level of technical skill.

Above the Godan rank are five more levels of *dan* rank, from the sixth, *Rokudan*, through the tenth, *Judan*. Mere technical competence is not enough to achieve these ranks; one must truly demonstrate that he lives a life dedicated to the pursuit of serious knowledge in karate-do. In most systems the holders of these ranks are considered to be masters. Many karate styles also designate these ranks by the use of belts that are red and white, solid red, or solid white. In others, like the Shotokan styles, all holders simply wear a black belt.

Holders of advanced rank are acknowledged in other ways in a seniority system. Just as in a military organization, holding rank brings with it certain privileges and responsibilities. When class begins, the students line up according to rank, with the highest grade on the right and lowest grade on the left of the line. Higher ranks are allowed to assist the instructor in teaching, as needed. They are also responsible for seeing that those under them are acting properly in the dojo.

There are ten *dan* grades. In ISKF/JKA all *dan* holders from one through ten wear black belts. In many organizations, grades one through five wear black belts; grades six, seven and eight wear red and white belts; and grades nine and ten wear red belts.

Shodan: first degree	black belt
Nidan: second degree	black belt
Sandan: third degree	black belt
Yondan: fourth degree	black belt
Godan: fifth degree	black belt
Rokudan: sixth degree	black belt in some organizations, red and white in others
Shichidan: seventh degree	black belt in some organizations, red and white in others
Hachidan: eighth degree	black belt in some organizations, red and white in others
Kudan: ninth degree	black belt in some organizations, red in others
Judan: tenth degree	black belt in some organizations, red in others

Conditioning

Age

As with any physical training regimen, age is an important factor. It generally takes about fifteen years for the average human brain to develop both hemispheres. This means that a fifteen-year-old should be able to successfully learn all of the techniques of karate. Younger children may take a longer period to learn, since their motor skills may not be fully developed. The younger the child, the more time it may take for him or her to gain proficiency in karate techniques. From a physical standpoint, this is acceptable, since karate training will assist in stimulating the brain to develop various motor skills.

Sports physicians consider athletes between the ages of fifteen and thirty-five to be the best candidates for karate training. Men over the age of thirty-five and women over the age of forty are considered to be old, as far as rigorous athletic training is concerned. There are always exceptions to be found, but this is the general opinion of the medical profession. Men in particular are more prone to heart problems and should undergo a good physical prior to beginning karate practice. Since their bodies are not in prime condition for learning karate, their progress will be slower than that of younger people.

Substance Abuse

Karate is a martial art but also an athletic endeavor. Therefore, one must be mindful of all aspects of body conditioning. Since we are practicing an art that requires complete self-control, any substance that alters our control over ourselves is unacceptable. Alcohol and drugs are primary enemies of good athletic conditioning. The deleterious effects of alcohol are widely known and need not be discussed here in any detail. If we are to keep ourselves physically fit, the avoidance of alcohol is a good idea. Overindulgence in beer in particular can put unwanted weight on our bodies. Drinking prior to practice is particularly dangerous, as we may not have the ability to control ourselves and may cause injury to ourselves or others. Showing up on the dojo floor smelling of alcohol is a sure way to get barred from the school. Your karate career may end very quickly if you do so. Any substance abuse counselor can tell you that alcohol is our most widely abused drug.

Illegal drugs come in a wide variety of substances, none of which is any good for us. In addition to limiting our control over ourselves and our conduct, they are addictive and can lead to serious health problems. Moreover, their use and possession can land you in jail. Karate should be practiced by people who avoid the use of drugs and alcohol.

Tobacco, both in the chewed and smoked form, poses another threat to health. Numerous studies have linked the use of tobacco to any number of health problems, from cancer to heart disease and many others. If we are going to place the extreme demands of karate training on our bodies, we need them to be in top shape.

Weight

In order to get the most from a training session, it is necessary to work as hard as possible and push ourselves to the limit. It goes without saying that the body must be in good condition in order for us to do this. Numerous charts exist that tell us what our ideal body weight should be. Although there is room for some variation, it is not difficult to determine when we are carrying too much weight. I normally try to keep myself at a certain body weight, around 175 pounds. The addition of ten pounds to my weight, or approximately 6 percent, is quite noticeable in the performance of technique. The loss of that much extra weight brings with it an increase in performance. Kicks and punches seem to have more speed and snap, and overall body movement is better. At one point during my contest years, I tried to bulk up to 190 pounds to see if that would give me an advantage. Although I felt strong, my movement was noticeably slower. Through experimentation, my ideal body weight for the performance of karate techniques was determined. In the same way, you must pay close attention to the messages that your body sends. If you feel slow and logy, you may be overweight. Experiment with some minor dieting to see the effects. That is the suggested method if you are only slightly overweight. If you are significantly overweight, then you must check with your physician to determine what kind of diet will be best for you. The use of diet pills and other weight reduction drugs should be strictly under the direction of a doctor.

Warming Up and Cooling Down

One cannot begin any serious physical exercise without a proper warmup. Karate training places great demands on the practitioner, and the body must be prepared for the increased physical activity. A normal karate training session begins with a warmup period and ends with a cooling down period. Let's look at the warmup first.

After the students and instructor bow in, they begin the training session with a warmup. These movements are done slowly at first and then increase in rapidity as the warmup progresses. One of the facets of this warmup is an increase in the heart rate. Prior to beginning training, you should have identified your maximum heart rate.

The purpose of the warmup is to reach your target heart rate prior to beginning intense physical activity. For most people, this may take from ten to twenty minutes. Begin your movements slowly by wobbling your body loosely and then your arms, legs, hands, and feet. This is known as the inside to out-

To find your maximum heart rate:

1. Subtract your age from 220. According to this formula, a twenty year old would have a maximum heart rate of 200, and a forty year old a maximum heart rate of 180.

2. Your target heart rate for training, as a beginner, will be between 50 percent and 70 percent of your maximum heart rate. It may reach as high as 90 percent for young, well-trained athletes in top condition.

side method. After doing that for a minute or so, begin to jump loosely, followed by about a minute or two of jumping jacks. At this point you will begin to feel your heart rate start to increase. Neck rotation and movement is next, followed by shoulder rotations and trunk movement. Turn your head to the right and then to the left and repeat the movement several times. Then bend your neck forward and backward and, finally, rotate your head several times. Bring your hands out in front of your body with your arms parallel to the floor. Pull both fists back to your sides in the preparatory position for the punch. Do this half a dozen times. With both arms extended, swing them to your sides at the same time. As you do this, they should be kept parallel to the floor. Bring both fists to your chest and twist your body alternately to the left and right, exercising the muscles of the trunk. Rotate your shoulder joints by swinging your arms in a circular movement, first forward, then with the rotation reversed. Place your left hand behind your back and your right overhead, and bend to the left side. Switch arm positions and bend to the right side. Repeat this about a dozen times. With your hands overhead, rotate your body, leaning forward, to the left, backward, and to the right. Rotate in both directions for several rotations. Now it is time to loosen the lower part of your body.

Assume the front stance, but in a lower position than normal for training. Place both hands against your lower back and push your hips forward as you lower your body. Do this on both sides. Lower your body on one side by extending one leg and bending the opposite knee sharply. Try to keep your heel flat on the floor and attempt to press the back of your extended leg's knee to the ground. Do this on both sides. Spread your legs as far apart as possible and try to do a side split. Switch from this into a front split, and then reverse to do the other side. Assume the sitting position on the floor with both legs spread as widely as possible. Touch your chest to your knees on both sides and then to the center. Bring your legs together and touch your forehead to your knees. Then, while still in a seated position, bring both feet in close to your body. Move your bent legs up and down, and then push down on your knees. Assume the standing position once again with your feet together. Rotate your knees in a circular movement, both to the right and left.

Having now moved and mildly stretched most parts of your body, you may begin to do some loose karate movements. Without using any speed and power, go through the basic straight punch and all six basic blocking motions in a standing position. Then practice the front kick, alternating from right to left. Do about twenty repetitions of each.

At this point, you should have been warming up for anywhere from five to ten minutes, depending how many repetitions of each exercise you do. You are now ready to begin the next phase of training. This involves actual karate technique, but for the first ten minutes or so of this part, you should not try to perform the techniques to the maximum. The emphasis here should be on form, rather than exertion. After about ten minutes of this type of light training, you may switch to more intensive exercises.

The above scenario for a warmup period in the training session is basic, with the understanding that age, experience, and general health factors will be the final determining factor on how long you need to warm up before your body is ready. If you find that the warmup run by the instructor at the beginning of practice is not sufficient, then get to the dojo a little earlier so that you may warm up at your own pace. Remember, the class may be very mixed, and the instructor may have to run a warmup suitable for most students but not necessarily sufficient for everyone.

After training for close to an hour, your heart rate may be well within the target heart rate zone and may need to be brought down to normal. The last part of training should consist of a set of exercises done with less intensity than the earlier movements, and you should feel your heart begin to slow. During this last phase, try to relax and bring the body down from its high point in exercise. Warm-downs may take more or less time for different people, but about ten minutes is a general time. If you find that the class warm-down is not sufficient, then move a bit more after class until your heart rate feels normal.

chapter 16
how to
participate in
a training session

I N ORDER TO GET THE MOST out of your workout, there are some basic rules to follow. First of all, your body is going to go through a strenuous training session, one that will require that it perform with peak efficiency. This means that it must be prepared. In chapter 15, we have covered the basic warmup procedures, so we will now address the actual participation in a training session.

Concentration and Focus

In classes aimed at beginners, the instructor will usually do a great deal of teaching. That is to say, good directions should be given in regard to how each technique is performed. The instructor will usually demonstrate the technique slowly, explain how it is used, and indicate particular points of which to be mindful. He will frequently use a student to assist him. If he is demonstrating an offensive technique, such as a kick or punch, the student will be a target. When showing a defensive technique, he will have the student punch or kick at him in order to demonstrate how the block works. When hearing this type of explanation, try to make sure that you follow the directions exactly and do the technique as the instructor directs. This is where your concentration is important.

You will hear instructors refer to the use of kime, or focus, a concept that is unique to karate. It was discussed briefly in chapter 8, but it bears some further explanation if you are to perform karate techniques perfectly. In order to move with speed, it is necessary for muscles to be relaxed. If you tense them, movement is slowed or made awkward. The only time your body is tensed is at the moment that you make contact with the opponent. At the moment of impact, all the muscles of your body must be tensed for a split second and then immediately relaxed. This may be applied to blocks, kicks, punches, and strikes. Once you have focused your technique on your opponent, you must relax instantly so that you may follow up with additional techniques if needed. If you fail to focus on the technique as it is being performed, it may not be powerful enough to stop your opponent. Let's examine why this is considered to be so important.

Karate originally developed as a weaponless fighting art. The primary reason for this was that it was for the people, not professional military men. Those in service to the feudal lord had ample supplies of weapons and the training to use them effectively. The populace was denied the possession of weapons in seventeenth-century Okinawa, so it was vital that they learn to defend themselves without weapons. In many cases, they would be using karate techniques against an opponent equipped with a sword or knife. In a situation such as that, the karate practitioner probably had only one chance to strike his opponent. If he missed, or if the technique was not strong enough to disable or kill his opponent, he would be cut down by the sword. There was only one chance to score. This has led to the practice of what the Japanese term *ikken-hisatsu*, which literally means "one-punch death blow." To develop your technique to the point that you can disable your opponent with one punch, kick, or strike takes great skill. When you go through training, concentrate on the techniques one at a time as you perform them. When doing a kata, for instance, make sure that you have completely executed each move with focus before moving on to the next one. We might add here that not all moves in the kata will have focus; some will simply be done smoothly and are transitional in nature.

Kime refers to the instantaneous tensing of muscles and the physical and psychological concentration on the target at the moment of impact.

In many of the sparring drills, such as one-step, three-step, and semifree-sparring, the offensive side attacks with one punch or kick, and the defensive side counters with a single technique. The idea here is that one should concentrate on the one technique in order to make it as strong as possible. Following up with several other kicks and punches simply indicates that you have no confidence in your ability to finish your opponent with one blow. This means that you need more practice.

Elements of the Training Session

Beginning Slowly

Let's go through the training session and look at some important points. Having begun with a general warmup and stretching routine, the class will begin training. Usually the first part of training is devoted to the practice of basic techniques, either singly or in combination. This will be determined by the instructor, based on the level of the students in the class. In many cases, you will be asked to perform the techniques slowly for the first part and then with speed and focus after that. The purpose in having you practice the movements slowly is to give you time to do them correctly. Pay particular attention at this point, since incorrect movement practiced for any length of time can be difficult to correct. An instructor's worst nightmare occurs when students enter the school after having trained with incompetent instructors. Their movement is frequently wrong, and the instructor must then try to make corrections, which proves frustrating to the student. This is why you must choose a good school to begin with. During practice, you may find that it is difficult to perform some techniques with speed and still do them correctly. For training purposes, it is much more important to do them correctly, even if you have to slow them down a bit to do so. Speed will come with repetition, but if the movement is incorrect, you will have problems in the future.

We have already discussed the use of focus in technique. Remember, as you practice, that punching power comes from speed, and the body cannot produce speed in movement if it is tensed. Keep your body "soft" between techniques, and you will be able to move quickly and efficiently. If you stand there with your body tensed, you will move slowly and tire rapidly. There is no need for tension in the body unless you are making contact with your opponent.

Applying Techniques

A second part of the karate class will probably be devoted to applying the techniques of blocking, punching, striking, and kicking against an opponent. This is accomplished through the use of various sparring drills. In these drills, which are usually prearranged, you will have the opportunity to concentrate on basic techniques, movements, timing, and focus. The basics of how to do these drills were covered in chapter 8.

There are many types of drills, each with a different emphasis. Although all give practice in balance and the execution of techniques, each has a specific skill that is considered most important in that drill. Earlier, we discussed distancing, timing, and related subjects in the one-step and three-step sparring drills. Direction reversing is another important skill to master. Make sure that you understand the skill to be learned in each type of drill and concentrate on it.

There are three main parts to every training session: warmups and basic techniques, applying techniques through sparring drills, and kata.

One of the features of these drills, frequently overlooked by students, is the beginning position for the defender. Under normal circumstances, if we are attacked, we probably will be standing in a normal upright position with the feet about one shoulders' width apart. This is the beginning position for both the attacker and defender in the basic drills. The attacker shifts from his normal everyday stance to a front stance in preparation for attack, and the defender must shift from his normal stance to a front stance to defend. This movement of shifting from normal positions to defensive positions is important and must be reinforced continually. This is one of the reasons why both participants in the drill come to the zanshin position after each set is performed. It reinforces the movement to defense.

The three drills noted above are only a few of many that skilled instructors have developed in order to teach their students the rudiments of karate movement. They are usually referred to as basic sparring drills, because the attack is prearranged and they focus on basic movement. Numerous others exist, some against one opponent and some against multiple opponents. Keep in mind that karate was not developed as a sport and that therefore you may have several opponents. As described in chapter 13, one drill that takes this into account has the defender standing in the zanshin position with one opponent in front of him and one to the rear. The opponent in front attacks, and, after he is blocked and countered, the opponent to the rear then launches his attack. Recall that another drill has four opponents—to the front, rear, left, and right. In these drills, one must make sure of the counterattack. Just as in a real fight, there is only one chance to finish an opponent before another is upon you.

More advanced students practice all of the drills mentioned above but also practice free-sparring. This may be done in slow motion, half speed or full speed. Slow-motion sparring gives you the chance to correct your technique, since there is little danger of injury if your opponent scores on you. It also allows the practice of techniques that might otherwise not be practiced if full speed were used. Half-speed sparring steps up the pace a bit, and full-speed free-sparring strains the student's ability to the limit. Full-speed sparring is best done under the watchful eye of an instructor, in order that the combatants do not get carried away and cause injuries to one another.

In full-speed sparring, there is little time to practice techniques and correct deficiencies. You are in a situation where you must fight as best you can. Normally, free-sparring at full speed is not practiced a great deal until around black-belt level. Students need to continue the development of their basic skills. The goal of all practice in basics, sparring drills, and kata is the ability to free-spar with speed and control. Accordingly, it is not the main method of practice for students below black-belt level. Higher-grade black belts may do some warmup kicks and punches and then go right into the practice of free-sparring, but their proficiency and level dictate that they will benefit from more free-sparring practice. One of the marks of an incompetent instructor is that he will have his students free-spar in the first few weeks of training, long before they have developed any control or competency in basic movement. Students trained in this manner will either drop out of the school or manage to hang on. The focus of their training will then be survival in sparring matches, and they will take shortcuts to do so. This will ensure that they do not develop the sound foundation in basic technique that will allow them to progress in the future. They will reach a certain level of proficiency and then be unable to progress, since their technique has never been developed properly. In short, you must first sit up, crawl, stand, and walk before you run. It is a natural progression in learning any physical movement, and shortcuts simply do not work.

In all of your practice, you must learn to coordinate your entire body. Let's look at the lunge punch, oi-zuki, as an example. There are two major components of this technique. One is the actual step forward as you move toward your opponent. The second is the movement of the arm as the fist is thrust forward. In order to develop maximum power in the lunge punch, one must coordinate the movement of the body with the movement of the hand. Done correctly, the step is completed just as the arm is straightened. This adds the power of the body's movement to the hand technique. This is common sense and a principle common to all athletic endeavors. In schools where the instructors do not have a complete grasp of the fundamentals, it is not uncommon to see them teach students to step, and then to execute the punch once the step has been completed. Establishing a solid foundation of basic techniques is one of the reasons that you need to find a good instructor.

Practicing Kata

The third part of the training session is the practice of kata. Beginning students always want to learn more kata, thinking that the more they know, the greater their karate ability. This is a mistake. It is far better to be skillful at one kata than to simply know the moves to five. In general, the sequence of kata to be learned follows a logical pattern. The first kata taught emphasize basic techniques along with large movements of the body. Intermediate kata require much more body control and development of technique, in order to be performed correctly. Advanced kata are the most difficult of all, with many containing acrobatic moves or slow movements that require exceptional body control. Students cannot perform the intermediate or advanced kata correctly unless they have put in enough training time to develop their basic movement. Do not be in a great rush to learn more kata. Your instructor will watch your movement progress and will teach you the next kata when you are ready.

When you practice a kata, make sure that you learn the correct sequence of moves first. After that, you need to learn the rhythm of the kata and its fine points. After you get the basic movements down, the moves need to be understood better. This is where the practice of bunkai comes in. Take each move in the kata and have a training partner attack you so that you can see how the movement works against an opponent. In many cases, the instructor will make this a regular part of the class, but, in other cases, you may practice it on your own after the training session has ended.

The various kata contain all the variations of body movement of which we are capable. Training in them is extremely important and will greatly improve your ability to spar and perform a variety of offensive and defensive movements with skill.

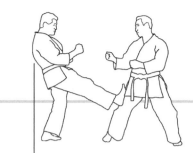

Developing Power

AS WE USE OUR BODIES to perform karate techniques, we find that there are three ways to develop power: (1) body shifting, (2) body rotation, and (3) body vibration. Let's see how they work.

Body Shifting

Body shifting is the most obvious of the movements used to develop power in karate technique. It is by this means that maximum power is developed in a kick, punch, or block. Body shifting implies that we are moving the body from one location to another, usually forward as we execute an attack. The most common of the karate techniques that involve this principle is the lunge punch. In this technique, the movement of the body as it is propelled forward toward the target is added to the power of the hand movement. This is much more powerful than simply standing in place and punching.

It is probably easiest to see the power in the body shift as we practice our front kick against a heavy bag. Stand in the left front stance and prepare to kick the bag with your rear foot. Kick the bag with your right foot and step back into your beginning stance. For comparison, kick the bag and step forward. It will be obvious that the kick utilizing the forward motion of the body is much more powerful than the kick in which the body has been relatively stationary.

Body Rotation

Body rotation is the second method of developing power using our bodies. In order to develop maximum power in the kick, punch, or block, it is necessary to understand and use correct hip movement and body rotation. Body rotation is more subtle than body shifting, since the movement is smaller. This type of movement should be very familiar to Americans, because we see it practiced in various sports continually. Let's look at the baseball player as he takes his turn at bat. For the purposes of our discussion, we will make him right-handed. He stands with his feet perpendicular to the path of the oncoming ball. His hips, therefore, are in line with the path as well. We can call this a side-facing position. As he begins his swing, he steps toward the pitcher and moves his left or forward foot outward and rotates his hips as he begins the swing of the bat. As he finishes the swing, his feet will probably be about one shoulders' width apart, and his hips will face directly toward the pitcher. In executing this type of body movement, it is obvious that he has used the rotation of his hips and body in order to give power to his swing. The hip rotation used in the baseball batter's swing is practically the same as that used by the karate practitioner in executing a reverse punch. Let's take a look at the reverse punch to see the similarities.

The three ways to develop strength are: body shifting, body rotation, and body vibration.

The karate practitioner stands in the left front stance. His left hand is in the downward blocking position, and his body in the side-facing position. This means that his hips are in line with the path that his fist will travel as it goes from his hip to the target. His punch begins with his hips being rotated counterclockwise toward the opponent. As they turn approximately one-half of the way forward, he begins the punch. His hip and fist both complete their movement at the same time. Neither the baseball batter nor the karate practitioner can get any power into his swing or punch without moving his hips. It would be ridiculous to imagine a batter trying to hit the ball without rotating his hips and body, and equally impossible to execute a strong punch without moving them. This type of hip rotation may be observed in other sports as well, among them the swing used as the golfer hits the ball.

We have described the use of body rotation as it applies to hand techniques—in the case above, the reverse punch. It is also used in kicking techniques such as the front, side, and roundhouse kicks. Let's see how it works. Stand in the left front stance with your hips to the side. Rotate your hips around and begin the front kick with your back leg. This will add the power of your hips to the kick, and it will be stronger than if you simply kicked with your hips facing the front. In the same stance, stand with your hips facing directly forward. This time kick with your front leg. As you raise your knee and begin the front kick, rotate your hips clockwise in order to add power to the kick. This type of rotation exists in all kicks, so you must pay attention to the movement of your hips as you execute all kicking techniques. Some people have stiff hip movement and cannot develop as much rotational power as others; however, it is a natural part of body movement, and thus everyone can do it to a greater or lesser extent.

One of the factors that helps to develop power through body and hip rotation is the principal of centrifugal force. This requires that the hips be rotated sharply with a snap, not just rotated in the direction of the kick, punch, or block. To understand how this works, stand in the left front stance with your arms hanging loosely at your sides. Your hips should be in the side-facing position. Slowly rotate your hips to the forward position. Your arms will move along with your hip movement but will not be extended far from your body. Try the same move again but this time snap your hips forward. If you keep your arms loose, you will notice that they will fly uncontrollably out from your body. This is the result of centrifugal force. It comes from speed in movement. In order to add centrifugal force to our punch or kick, it is necessary to snap the hips around as we do a technique, not just slowly rotate them.

Body Vibration

The third and most subtle of the means of developing power is body vibration. Simply put, this implies that all the muscles of the body are tensed at the moment of impact. It is difficult to see any movement in the body as this takes place, since it is more of an internal than an external process. This type of power-developing method is used primarily when it is difficult to shift or rotate the body, as in the case of close quarters. The only method available will be the rapid tensing of the muscles as the punch is delivered. Techniques such as the hook punches in the kata *Tekki Shodan* are good examples of power generated through body vibration.

Strength Training

Let's begin to talk about strength from a practical point of view. How strong do you have to be in order to practice karate well? It certainly does not hurt to be strong, but will strength necessarily improve your karate technique? The answer here is no. Ours is a fighting art, not one in which we have to lift heavy objects or present the image of strength by the appearance of our muscles. What we need more than strength is speed and timing. Any improvement in our karate is going to come from repetition of the movements, not from increased strength. This does not mean that weight training cannot be beneficial; all sports encourage weight training to build overall strength. We just have to be careful that any strength-training exercises supplement our karate training and do not compromise our technique. Weight training should be focused on the muscle groups that enhance the movements required to excel in a particular athletic activity.

Traditional karate schools have always used various pieces of training equipment to increase strength. Among them are *chashi*, which are small, hand-held weights with handles. They are used to develop strength in various punches and blocks. Iron *geta*, worn on the feet, are used to develop leg strength. Pots, or *kame*, with a wide mouth, are filled with stones or other weights and used to develop the grip. Other pieces of equipment are used as well, such as the heavy club. This is swung from overhead or the side and then stopped in front of the body. Most of these devices were traditionally home-made, and newer types of dumbbells and weights are more practical for today's practitioner.

Let's begin with some general exercises of a calisthenic nature. Push-ups and sit-ups are pretty basic. However, it is important that we do them in a way that will help our technique, not hinder it. Push-ups designed to build impressive pectoral muscles are not of great use to us. We need to strengthen them, but the triceps muscle in our arm is more important. Therefore, when you do push-ups, keep your arms and elbows close in to your sides, with your palms on the floor about one shoulders' width apart. This will work the triceps muscles at the back of the arms more than the pectoral muscles of the chest. In effect, you will be duplicating the punching movement, only with resistance. Push-ups are normally done with the palm on the dojo's wooden floor, but it is more beneficial if we do them using our fists. Make sure that the fist is tight, the wrist straight, and the weight squarely on the first two knuckles and fingers. This will be uncomfortable in the beginning, but you will be strengthening your wrist and hand for punching. This hardening of the striking knuckles will make the makiwara training more efficient. Thirty repetitions of this type of push-up is sufficient for beginners, but the number should be increased as strength is developed.

Sit-ups may be done in a variety of ways. For our purposes, it is important that the legs be bent at the knees and not kept straight. Internal muscles that connect the pelvis to the upper leg will be tightened if the legs are kept straight. This will decrease flexibility—not a good thing for karate practitioners.

Strong stomach muscles are important for those who practice karate. They help to raise the upper leg in kicking motions and, if strengthened, may provide protection against kicks and punches to the midsection. Fifty repetitions of sit-ups at a time are a good number to aim for, although more will certainly not hurt. Done on a daily basis, these will have a positive effect on technique. Try to work up to four sets of fifty sit-ups. Proper use of a medicine ball will also help build strong stomach muscles.

We have already discussed connection as it relates to the performance of your technique. This simply means that your entire body moves as one unit, with the lower portion and the upper working together. Strong abdominal muscles play a vital role in one's ability to transmit body power into hand techniques. The upper body is protected by the rib cage. The only skeletal feature between the upper body and the pelvic girdle is the backbone. This means that support for the midsection of the body comes from various muscles. The abdominal muscles, being in the front of the body and far removed from the backbone, are extremely important.

Another factor makes tight abdominals imperative for anyone performing kicking movements. The abdominal muscles form a connection between the rib cage and the pelvic bones and keep the pelvis aligned correctly. When the abdominal muscles are out of shape, the pelvis tilts forward. Since the sciatic nerve runs from the backbone through a hole in the pelvic girdle and then down the leg, it will be affected. As the pelvis tilts forward, the nerve is pinched and some pain may occur. In normal activities this is uncomfortable; however, during kicking the effect is intensified. Sit-ups and other abdominal exercises that tighten the muscles will alleviate the problem.

Training equipment used in traditional schools may include chashi, which are hand-held weights; iron geta, which are sandles made out of iron; kame, which are wide-mouthed pots filled with stones; and the heavy club.

Numerous other calisthenic types of exercise exist and can be helpful in building overall body strength. Jumping jacks, squat thrusts, and various other movements can have a beneficial effect. These exercises all involve moving several muscle groups rather than isolated ones.

In order to gain maximum strength, the use of weights is necessary. These may be of a free-weight variety, or the effect may be simulated through the use of various resistance-type exercise machines and devices. Let's consider using free weights, since they are traditional. Resistance devices usually replicate the same movements. Lifts that require explosive speed are the best exercises, since this is an essential skill for karate movement. Two of the most useful are the two-hand snatch and the clean and jerk. In order to perform these particular lifts one must move very quickly, with resistance provided by the weights. They also provide overall exercise for the body, since the muscles of the arms, shoulders, back, and legs must all be used. In short, they are overall body exercises, not ones aimed at specific muscle groups. If we are to strengthen our bodies as a supplemental exercise, then we should use whole-body exercises. There are numerous other exercises that may be utilized, including squats, bench presses, toe raises, military presses, and leg curls. Be sure to get qualified instruction before attempting these lifts.

The number of repetitions to do of a specific exercise is always in question. In order to build strength, one usually uses high weight and low repetitions. Using light to medium weights and high repetitions tends to pump up muscles, but muscle mass is not the objective of strength training. The karate practitioner needs a combination of strength and speed, not bulk.

The type of body that one has is a result of heredity. While weight training or martial arts training can modify the body somewhat, it is impossible to change one's genetic makeup and body type. As a result, most people who are thin and wiry may increase their strength but will not see great increases in their size. What we can do, however, is modify the way in which our body utilizes our muscles.

The human body has two basic types of muscle fiber, red and white. Red muscle fiber is referred to as "slow twitch" and the white as "fast twitch." Red muscle fibers have high endurance and contract slowly. White muscle fibers have low endurance but contract much faster. Scientists believe that the percentages of each are determined through genetics. Weight training utilizes red fibers more than white fibers, so one may logically conclude that weight training by itself will not increase the speed of one's technique. It will, however, allow for greater endurance if the muscles are trained properly. This is seen as one of the beneficial results of weight training.

Although the practice of karate involves quick movement, a certain amount of endurance is necessary as well. This is particularly necessary if the fight lasts more than a few minutes. The longer the fight goes on, the more the body will rely on endurance. Endurance and stamina can be increased through arduous karate training, distance running, and the use of a jump rope.

Karate Training Equipment

All athletic activities have specific equipment that assists the practitioner in achieving proficiency. In karate, there are two pieces of equipment that are common, the makiwara and the heavy bag. Both of these are useful in developing technique. The makiwara, or punching board, is perhaps the one unique piece of equipment to be found in the dojo. It is designed to aid in the development of power in the punch, strike, or kick. The makiwara is a post about four feet high that is tapered near the top. Various models have been developed over the years. The original makiwaras were about eight feet long, with the bottom four feet buried in the ground. Modern makiwaras usually are set

The *makiwara* is a punching board used in karate training.

into metal brackets and bolted to the dojo floor. Various thicknesses of wood may be used, but the key is to keep the makiwara flexible. The makiwara must have enough flexibility that it can be punched with maximum power. Only in that way will it be useful in developing the punch, strike, or kick. The most common technique trained on the makiwara is the reverse punch, although any technique may be practiced. It is important to train both sides of the body, not just the favorite side. In fact, it is beneficial to train one's weaker side with greater intensity, in order to make both sides equal in power. Since most karate techniques are practiced by striking an imaginary opponent and punching and kicking the air, makiwara training is essential to develop the feeling of impact. The karate practitioner who avoids the makiwara will limit his or her development.

The mark of a karate enthusiast has always been a set of large knuckles, developed through training on the makiwara. Sometimes individuals forget that the makiwara is used to develop the punch, and think that because they have large knuckles they are karate experts. Training in the makiwara should be reserved for mature students whose bones are completely formed. Usually, intense makiwara training should not take place until at least the age of sixteen. The bones of young children are not strong enough, and training on the makiwara too early may cause irreparable damage.

A second type of equipment commonly seen in the dojo is the heavy or medium bag. Students may practice their kicks, punches, or strikes against it. A hundred-pound bag suspended from the ceiling is best. Other varieties of equipment have been developed in recent years, including air-filled bags that the instructor can hold, punching mitts that can be used as targets, basketball-sized inflated balls on stretch cables, and so on. Many of these devices have been borrowed from the sports world and have proven useful.

Mental Training

Traditional karate is not fun and games, it is serious business. In order to be successful, you must approach it in a mature manner. Let's consider the mental aspects of your training.

When you first enter the dojo, you will bow to the photos of the past masters on the wall and to your instructor if he is present. This is done as a sign of respect for those who have passed before as well as a greeting to the instructor. If you are early, there will be some free time before class so that you can practice your technique. You are expected to engage in some self-training once you are on the floor. The dojo floor is not a place for horseplay or joking around; it is a place to be serious. Normally, the instructor will not be on the floor unless it is almost time to train. When the instructor enters the training area, students are expected to face him and bow in greeting. The senior student will then call for the class to line up. Be sure to move quickly and get in line.

The instructor or instructors will line up in front of the students' line, facing the photos of the past masters or founder. The chief instructor will kneel and assume the meditation position. The senior student will then call "*seiza*," at which time the students will kneel in the same manner. Once all are in the kneeling position, the senior student will then call "*mokuso*." This is the command to meditate. Your mental training begins here in earnest. Relax and try to clear your mind of all your concerns so that it will be able to concentrate on the training. If you have had problems at work, or family concerns, these must be blanked out in order that you may be mentally prepared for the training session. Concentrate on deep breathing. After a few minutes of meditation, you will hear the command to end the meditation ses-

Listen for these calls from the senior student: *seiza*, which is the signal to kneel; *mokuso*, which is the signal to meditate; *mokuso-yame*, which is the signal to stop meditating; *Shinzen-ni rei*, which is the signal to bow to the photo of the founder of karate; *Sensei-ni rei*, which is the signal to bow to your instructor.

sion, "*mokuso-yame*." Students and instructor then bow to the photo of the founder upon the command "*Shinzen-ni rei*." Once this has been completed, the instructor will turn and face the students, and they will bow to each other. To indicate this, the senior student will call "*Sensei-ni rei*." The instructor may say a few words about the class or give another message of greeting, and then all will rise and begin training.

Once you have arisen and gone through the warmup period, you will line up and go through various drills. As each one ends, you will be given the order "yame," or stop. When you hear this command, you return to the zanshin position, in which you will stand in one of the informal attention stances. During this entire time, you must concentrate on an imaginary opponent in front of you. This is the essence of mental training, the concentration on an opponent. As you stand in zanshin, or proceed through the drills, imagine an opponent in front of you at all times. Those who can concentrate and do this will gain far more from the training session than those who do not. If you can see and feel this imaginary opponent, then the punches, kicks, and blocks thrown into thin air take on a sense of reality that will benefit you greatly.

In a formal training session, the students will move back and forth to the instructor's commands and perform various techniques that he directs. This is a good time to practice reaction timing. Hold yourself in position until you hear the instructor's voice command, then instantly perform the next karate movement. Training in this manner enforces stimulus/response activity in the brain and will help you to react to an opponent's attack. If you try to anticipate the voice command and move too soon, or disregard it and move too late, you will not be training properly.

An important part of training for actual self-defense involves developing your fighting spirit. This is a difficult part of the training session, and, if the instructor engages in it, some students will be discouraged, but those who persist will gain an important advantage. If we observe matches in any combative art—boxing, Olympic style wrestling, or karate—we will notice that as the match proceeds, the combatants tire. If the match proceeds long enough, both fighters will be so exhausted that they will hardly be able to execute their techniques. In this case, the one who has the stronger spirit will prevail. The loser will basically give up. Remember, one of the objectives of combat is to break your opponent's will to fight. In order to develop this kind of spirit, there will be times when you must perform to the point of exhaustion and then continue to train further. This may be impossible to do on your own, and your instructor may have to push you beyond your limits. After you have been pushed beyond your limits many times, your spirit will grow stronger as you attain these higher plateaus, and you will not lose your fighting spirit. This translates into not losing your life when faced with opponents who are trying to take it. Developing fighting spirit is an important and essential part of karate training, and the rewards are great.

Not every training session will involve spirit training, although many will be challenging. It is this constant push to your limits that will make you grow. Think in terms of the weightlifter who lifts the same two-hundred-pound weight in every exercise. He cannot grow very much unless he tries to lift more. Your karate training must be the same way—you must challenge yourself. A good instructor will help you to do this.

It goes without saying that such training requires that you be in top physical and mental condition, and it is most suitable for those who are younger. Older students must approach this type of training with great care, making sure that they are mentally sound and in good physical health.

Let's consider our mental state as we approach combat. One of the most famous swordsmen of old Japan was Miyamoto Musashi. In addition to killing many men in sword fights, he was also an artist and philosopher. His book *Gorin no Sho*, or the *Book of Five Rings*, has been well known for centuries. It is available in bookstores even today, due to the popularity of martial arts. In his work, Musashi describes the state of mind needed in order to develop winning skills in fighting. According to him, one must constantly think of winning.

There should be no inner vision of losing to another. Look at each possible opponent and imagine yourself defeating him. Never imagine yourself defeated. As you meet new people on the street or in the dojo, think always how, if necessary, you could score on them. Imagine how each kick or punch will get through their defenses and how they will fall under your attack. Constantly visualizing yourself as a winner is essential.

Achieving the correct state of mind is paramount if we are to win our battles. What shall we concentrate on when we face our opponent? Shall our mind be preoccupied with thoughts of specific techniques to attack him or defensive maneuvers if he attacks first? In his instructive essay to the famed swordsman Munenori Yagyu (1571–1646), the Zen priest Takuan (1573–1645) advised him on how to control his mind. According to Takuan, the mind should be clear and not fixed on any thoughts. If you fix your mind on the opponent's sword, you will be distracted by it. Allowing your mind to focus on any particular aspect of the enemy or yourself will cause you to be distracted. What is needed is the state of *mushin*, or no-mind. In this state, the mind is perfectly clear and undistracted. It can correctly perceive the opponent's actions and will allow the body to respond instantly. There will be no preexisting thought to get in the way.

Many Zen ideas are connected with the Japanese martial arts. One of the most common is the concept of *mizu no kokoro*, "a mind like water." This concept is similar to the no-mind of Takuan's admonition in that the mind must be like a calm pool of water, whose surface reflects all. If the mind is that clear, then the enemy's actions will be perceived at once. Achieving the type of mental state described here requires many years of concentrated practice, and few who begin karate training will achieve it.

EVERYONE who begins karate training has a reason for doing so. Some individuals simply want to get some exercise, while others want to delve deeply into the art and master it over a lifetime of training. On occasion, people have been the victims of physical assault, or know someone who has been attacked, and want to learn self-defense. In any dojo, people will have a variety of reasons for engaging in training. How about you? Why do you want to begin training?

Let's begin by setting a goal. This must be a realistic goal, based not only on your age and physical ability but on your available time. Younger people, who are unmarried or in jobs that do not require a great deal of responsibility, have the most time to train. They may be able to attend practice every day, and this

Keep your expectations and goals realistic and in line with your age, physical condition, and available training time.

daily training, coupled with their youth, will allow them to make rapid progress. Once people have other responsibilities, such as increased hours on the job, children, and family concerns, the amount of time available to train is much less. This means that advancement in rank and the attainment of proficiency in karate will take longer.

In chapter 5, we discussed when children should begin karate and noted that they probably should be at least six years of age. But how old can you be to begin karate training? The good news is that anyone in reasonable physical condition can train in karate. If you are sixty years old and beginning training, do not expect to fly through the air as though you were eighteen. Your expectations and goals must be realistic and in line with your age and condition. As long as we have mentioned condition, let's discuss that. If you have been physically active all your life, there is no reason that you cannot begin training in karate. However, common sense dictates that before starting any new physical training regimen, you have a good checkup. Tell your doctor what you plan to do and make sure that you are physically able to exercise.

Sometimes people say that they are not good athletes or are too stiff to perform karate techniques. They may be physically incapable of performing as if they were young athletes, but they can still do basic techniques. It does not matter if you are tall or short, skinny or overweight, old or young, male or female. Whatever your body type or condition, if you are attacked, you will have to defend yourself. Through knowledge of karate techniques, it will still be possible to save yourself from harm, no matter what your physical state.

Let's assume that you want to practice karate for physical conditioning. That is a good idea, and karate dojos are full of people training for just the same reason. The variety of exercises and the mental concentration required make karate a much better form of exercise than jogging in the park or putting miles on the treadmill. Karate training is about fifty/fifty aerobic/anaerobic exercise. If exercise is your reason for training, then you should be attending at least three classes a week. Training every day would be even better. You may be able to work out a schedule where you train several times during the week in the dojo and then self-train one or two days at home. It is a good idea not to self-train for the first few weeks, however, since you may develop bad habits without an instructor to watch your movements. After you have correct basic movement, you should try to practice at home whenever you cannot get to the dojo. If competition is your goal, then you should realize that, in every type of athletic competition, those who win train a great deal.

If karate is simply one of several forms of exercise in which you engage, and you like the variety of exercises, then training in karate once or twice a week will work for you. Just be mindful that this is a minimal training schedule, and you will not make rapid progress. The achievement of rank requires a certain commitment. Nevertheless, dojos are full of people who train occasionally, enjoy the activity greatly, and do not worry about attaining any particular rank.

The schedule on page 152 is suggested for a beginners' class consisting of individuals of mixed age and ability. If students have followed this training

Beginner's Training Schedule
(Three Classes per Week of One-Hour Duration)

Week	Basics	Sparring	Kata
1	Natural stance, front stance, lunge punch, reverse punch, downward block, front kick	None	None
2	Add rising block, outside forearm block	Three-step sparring	None
3	Add straddle stance, inside forearm block, back-fist strike, side snap-kick	Three-step sparring	None
4	Add back stance, knife-hand block, side thrust-kick	Add one-step sparring	Heian Shodan
Weeks 5–12	Continued practice of the techniques noted above	Continued practice of one- and three-step sparring drills	Continued practice of Heian Shodan

schedule for the three-month period, they should be ready to take the first examination for eighth kyu rank. Students wishing to gain great proficiency in karate would train twice as much, with training on six of the seven days of the week. Training sessions for them would be from one and a half to two hours long, and of greater intensity. Such classes are suitable for younger people or those in excellent physical condition.

A final note on the study of karate is appropriate here. We have discussed karate as self-defense and exercise, but there is another more important role that karate may play in your life. If approached properly, karate will provide an excellent means of physical and psychological growth. Challenging yourself to constantly perfect your movement and to push on in spite of physical discomfort has a beneficial effect on the spirit. Developing the ability to endure is probably the most important benefit of karate training, as the mental attitude developed through intense karate training will carry through to other aspects of the practitioner's life.

testing for rank

THE NORMAL SEQUENCE of training is for beginning students of karate to concentrate on basic movement, such as stances, blocks, kicks, and punches for the first few lessons. Then a basic sparring drill is introduced, such as one- or three-step sparring, which teaches the elements of distancing and timing. After students are familiar with the basic movements, usually requiring a couple of weeks, the first kata may be introduced.

Continued training in the basics over a period of a year or so will give students a good sense of control and understanding of the techniques. More advanced sparring drills will be introduced and several more kata added to the practice regimen. During this period, students should advance through the belt ranks. If they have trained regularly and learned the basics, they should be around green- to purple-belt level. Another half to full year of training would see them ranked as brown belts and reasonably capable of free-sparring without causing injury to themselves or others. These times are approximate, as we have not identified the number of training sessions per week that these students are attending. It is said that to become a black belt takes two years of training under a good instructor. This can be misleading. Two years of training seven days a week will get one to that goal. If a student trains only two or three times per week, it will take proportionately longer.

The Ranking Systems

Every karate organization has its own rank system, and there is great variety among the lower ranks. Let's begin with a discussion of the rank system. There are two types of rank, *kyu* and *dan*. Kyu ranks run downward from eight to one, so that the first rank a beginner can achieve is eighth kyu, although some schools also have a ninth and tenth kyu. The belts associated with these ranks differ according to the organization's practice. The most standard are the brown-belt ranks, which begin with third kyu and go to first kyu, which is one step away from the black-belt, or dan, ranks. For instance, the International Shotokan Karate Federation uses a yellow belt for eighth kyu, an orange belt for seventh kyu, and a green belt for sixth kyu. Purple belts are worn by fifth and fourth kyu holders. Brown belts are worn by those who are ranked from third kyu to first kyu. After you have attained the rank of first kyu brown belt, your next exam will be for the first level of black belt, which is known as Shodan. Dan ranks proceed upward from one to ten, with the higher ranks reserved for

> The kyu belt colors in karate are:
>
> ☞ Yellow: 8 kyu
>
> ☞ Orange: 7 kyu
>
> ☞ Green: 6 kyu
>
> ☞ Purple: 5 kyu and 4 kyu
>
> ☞ Brown: 3 kyu, 2 kyu, and 1 kyu

those who have trained in karate for a very long time. In many organizations, dan holders from one through ten, Shodan through Judan, wear black belts. In some styles, ranks of sixth, seventh, and eighth dan wear a red and white belt, while ninth and tenth dans wear a solid red belt. Some organizations vary this with a stripe in the belt, so you may encounter some different belt colors when you meet with instructors. In some schools, the lower ranks get stripes on their white belts to signify progress.

When you begin training, you wear a white belt and have no rank at all until your first exam. At that time, you will be tested and rank awarded according to your progress. Notice that promotion is based on your progress in learning karate techniques. We might have an eighteen-year-old athlete and a sixty-year-old grandfather take the same exam. Both may achieve the same grade. Will they look the same? Common sense dictates the answer here. What will be recognized is that each has made satisfactory progress according to his age and ability and that they have met a basic standard. Although you must meet these standards for knowledge and proficiency in technique, you are judged against yourself, not others.

The Exams

The Requirements

Tests for ranks from the kyu grades through the third degree of black belt, *San-dan*, usually have three parts. They are (1) the performance of basic techniques and combinations, (2) the performance of kata appropriate to the rank, and (3) sparring drills or free-sparring, jiyu-kumite. Tests for fourth degree, *yondan*, and above usually just include kata and free-sparring.

Let's begin by looking at the general idea behind each level of exam. Tests for the lower kyu grades are designed to reveal if you have grasped the basic concept behind the karate movements and learned to perform them appropriately, given your level of practice. The examiners are very concerned that you get off to a good start and that your knowledge of the movements will allow you to make satisfactory progress in the future. They are usually less concerned with how fast you can punch or kick than with how well balanced your stances are and the correctness of your hip movement.

Those testing for higher kyu rank will exhibit increased speed and strength in the basic techniques, the ability to perform them in combination, and also the ability to apply them satisfactorily against an opponent. While lower kyu ranks will perform basic sparring drills, those testing for the higher brown-belt ranks will usually perform semifree- or free-sparring. In these sparring drills, candidates must demonstrate appropriate advances in mastering the basic elements of fighting, such as distancing, reaction time, and so on. For each rank the appropriate kata must be performed.

After you have progressed through the kyu ranks, your instructor may invite you to test for the first degree of black belt, or Shodan. The test is designed to see if you have mastered the basic movements of karate. Conferral of the Shodan degree means just that—it does not mean that you have become an expert. Karate practitioners throughout the world realize that this is the first step in really learning karate. Sixty percent of the emphasis for this exam is on the performance of basic techniques and combinations. The remaining 40 percent is based on kata and kumite techniques. Passing the Shodan exam means that you have the basic tools, and now you must learn to put them to use.

One of the features of the Shodan exam is that you will be asked to free-spar. You have practiced this in your dojo and may have entered some competitions, but this will be different. You may lose your match but still pass the test and get the degree. This is because you are not being compared with anyone else during the test, only with yourself. Let's examine how this works. Suppose you are an average-sized person and you are called to spar with someone who is smaller and lighter. You will be expected to use your superior size and weight against your opponent. All other things being equal, the smaller person may be able to outmaneuver you, so if you try to play your opponent's game, it is a sign that you do not understand how to apply the basics to your own body type.

These are the kyu exams given by the International Shotokan Karate Federation. Other groups will have varying requirements, and the kata requirements will certainly be different.

Rank Requirements for Kyu Exams

Rank Belt	Color	Kihon	Kata	Kumite
8 Kyu	Yellow	Front stance, back stance, rising block, inside forearm block, outside forearm block, downward block, knife-hand block, front kick	Heian Shodan	Three-step sparring
7 Kyu	Orange	As above, add straddle stance, side snap-kick, and side thrust-kick	Heian Nidan	Three-step sparring
6 Kyu	Green	Add block-punch combinations, triple punch combination	Heian Sandan	One-step sparring
5 Kyu	Purple	Add roundhouse kick and consecutive front kicks	Heian Yondan	One-step sparring
4 Kyu	Purple	As above	Heian Godan	One-step sparring
3 Kyu	Brown	As above with increased ability to perform combination techniques	Tekki Shodan	One-step sparring
2 Kyu	Brown	As above	Bassai Dai	Semifree-sparring
1 Kyu	Brown	As above	Choice of Bassai Dai, Kanku Dai, Empi, Jion	Semifree-sparring

If you fight a larger person and try to stand against him instead of shifting out of his line of movement, this is another sign that you don't understand fighting strategy. Either of these flaws may cause you to fail the test.

During the exam for second and third degree black belt, Nidan and Sandan, you will be expected to exhibit increased ability in kata and kumite. Those passing the Sandan exam will have demonstrated that they have developed their own unique style based on mastery of the basic techniques. In other words, they have adapted karate to their own body type.

It is a widely held belief among karate practitioners that everyone can achieve Sandan if they continue to train over a lengthy period of time. The break between average performance and knowledge begins with fourth and fifth degree, *Yondan* and *Godan*. These are considered to be high grades, and those achieving them will have to have technique and knowledge far beyond the average. Up to this point, grades are awarded strictly on the basis of physical performance. Those achieving Godan rank are considered to have attained the maximum physical performance from their bodies.

Still another requirement is placed on those seeking rank of Yondan and above. A special research project focusing on some physical aspect of karate movement is required. This must be submitted in the form of a written report. On the day of the exam, the examinee is asked to demonstrate what he has researched and show how it applies in kumite.

Grades from six through ten, Rokudan through Judan, have other requirements associated with them. They include an increased ability to refine and develop new techniques and training methods, as well as the ability to teach others. Contributions to the art of karate and complete dedication to it are also prime considerations. These are not ranks for the occasional practitioner, but for those who have dedicated their lives to mastering the art. To achieve ranks above Godan takes many years of training, and those possessing them are usually in their late thirties or older. The higher ranks, such as eighth degree, *Hachidan*, and above are frequently reserved for practitioners above the age of sixty. As we noted earlier in this book, such high ranks held by men in their twenties are highly questionable.

Taking Your First Test

After you have trained for several months, you may be asked by your instructor to test for rank. Notice that I have said that you will be asked, not that you will ask. Your instructor will watch your progress and, when he feels that you

Rank Requirements for Dan Exams

Rank	Kihon	Kata	Kumite
Shodan	Various combinations of kicks, punches, and blocks	Tokui-kata from Bassai Dai, Kanku Dai, Empi, Jion plus examiner's choice from Heian 2–5 or Tekki Shodan	Free-sparring under the age of 45; over 45 the examinee has the choice of free-sparring or self-defense
Nidan	Various combinations of kicks, punches, and blocks	Tokui-kata plus examiner's choice from Bassai Dai, Kanku Dai, Empi, or Jion	As above
Sandan	Various combinations of kicks, punches, and blocks	Tokui-kata plus examiner's choice from Bassai Dai, Kanku Dai, Empi, Jion, Jitte, Hangetsu, Gankaku, Tekki Nidan, Tekki Sandan	As above
Yondan	Special research project written and demonstration	As above	As above
Godan	As above	As above	As above

have learned enough to progress to the next level, he will tell you that it is time to take a test.

You will probably be taking a test with others for the same or more advanced rank. Get to the dojo early enough to allow yourself a good warmup. You will want to be nice and loose, since you will not have a great deal of time to warm up once the test begins. In a first test, the examiner wants to see if you have grasped the basic fundamentals of the stance, block, kick, and punch. He will

Examiner Requirements for Exams
(International Shotokan Karate Federation Requirements)

Category	Examiners Required
Kyu exams	1A, 1B, 1C, 2D, and higher
Shodan	1A, 3B, 2B + 2C, and higher
Nidan	1A, 4B, and higher
Sandan	1A, 5B, and higher
Yondan	2A and higher
Godan	4A and higher

It should be noted that minimum requirements exist for examiner rankings. In addition to holding ranks as official instructors and tournament judges, the examiner must hold dan ranks as follows:

A Class Examiner minimum rank: Shichidan (seventh dan)

B Class Examiner minimum rank: Rokudan (sixth dan)

C Class Examiner minimum rank: Yondan (fourth dan)

D Class Examiner minimum rank: Sandan (third dan)

pay particular attention to your hip movement, balance, and posture, as well as your knowledge of dojo etiquette and your spirit. It is natural to be nervous. The feeling of butterflies in your stomach is a sign that your body is gearing up for the challenge. Once you actually begin to move, the butterflies will disappear and you will be performing your technique.

Let's look at the standard beginner's test as given by the International Shotokan Karate Federation. Again, those given by other organizations will vary, so the following should be considered as representative.

The exam begins with a lineup, meditation, and bow, just like a regular class. A senior student will lead the warmup. It will probably not be a long one, which is why it is good to get on the floor before the exam, to get your body ready. At this point, the examiner or an assistant instructor may explain what you are to do. On the floor will be several starting marks. Students taking the exam are called up, two or three at a time, and go to their assigned marks. They bow to the examiner, announce their names, and then face forward in the direction they will be moving.

The first part of the exam will let the examiner see your basic front stance, back stance, and basic blocks. He will also look

I t is not considered proper karate etiquette to demand of your instructor a timetable for your testing. If you don't have that much confidence in your instructor's powers of observation, then perhaps you chose the wrong instructor.

at your front kick. You will be told to assume the downward block position in the front stance, gedan-barai in zenkutsu-dachi. The first technique will be the lunge punch, oi-zuki, stepping forward. After several repetitions of this, counted by the examiner, you will be told to move backward and perform the rising block, age uke. Again, you will do several repetitions until you have reached the starting mark again. You will then step forward and perform the outside forearm block, soto-uke, several times. These three techniques have been performed in the front stance. Now it is time to check your knife-hand block and back stance. The examiner will have you move backward in the back stance, kokutsu-dachi, and perform the knife-hand block, shuto-uke. You will then return to the ready position. Once more you will be instructed to assume the front stance, and the examiner will have you step forward and perform the front snap-kick, mae-geri-keage. After several repetitions, you will turn and do several more to return to the starting point. After turning, you will be told to recover into the ready position. Now it is time to demonstrate your kata.

Usually the kata starting marks are in a different place. The examiner wants to see your basic techniques from the side, but will want you to face him to perform the kata. Assume the ready position at the mark, bow to the examiner, and announce your kata. Since it is your first test, it will be Heian Shodan. You will be told to begin. If others are doing their kata at the same time, do not pay any attention to them—make believe that they are not there. It doesn't matter who finishes first, it is not a race. What does matter is that you perform the movements correctly, with good balance and technique. Frequently the person who finishes first does the poorest kata. You must perform according to your own body type, not someone else's. When you have done the last movement in Heian Shodan, wait until the examiner calls "yame." You then return to the starting point and bow to the examiner. This finishes the first and second parts of the test, and you will be told to sit down.

In the third part of the test, you will demonstrate your ability to apply the techniques against an opponent in the three-step sparring drill. In addition to showing that you can block a punch and counterattack, you will be judged on your ability to understand an essential element in fighting, which is distancing. When you and your partner are called to the floor, both of you will face the examiner and bow, then bow to one another. One of you will be told to assume the downward block position in the front stance. If it is you, make sure that you have the correct distance between you and your opponent so that you may reach him with a single step. Assuming a position that is too close or too far away is considered a flaw, and you will lose points. If your opponent is to attack first and is too far away, do not help your attacker by moving forward to adjust the distance. If he is too close, you may move back to an appropriate distance. The drill you are demonstrating will probably only be performed on one side, so pick your favorite side and then get ready. When you are on the defensive side, be sure to kiai as you execute your counter. Make sure that you have adjusted your distance in the three steps so that you are close enough to your opponent to make contact, as if you were actually fighting. Distancing for the attacker and defender in this drill is most important, and you will be expected to make whatever adjustments are necessary. The first series of attacks is to the face, and the defender uses age-uke to block and then counters with gyaku-zuki. The second set is to the midsection, and the defender blocks with soto-uke.

The basic test described above is similar to that given in many karate schools. There will certainly be some variety between organizations. When you are taking your second or third test, the examiner may wish to see something specific and ask you to do additional techniques. If you have been training a great deal more than the others going for the same rank, you may also be asked to do the next kata. Maybe you joined the school a month after a regular exam and did not qualify to take the next one, since you did not have the required time in training. If the exams are regularly held every three months, this would mean that you have five months in training, but the other students who are taking the first test have trained for three months. Under such circumstances, you may achieve a higher rank than the others who are taking the test.

After you finish the test, you may think that you did not perform as well as you do in practice, but it is probably not true. You will perform on the test just as you do in regular training, in spite of your nerves. The examiner may make some general comments about the examinees at the end of the test, so pay close attention. The new grades will be announced within a few days, after the examiner has had a chance to review your performance and your training record. If you have not made any mistakes and have done well, you will probably be promoted to eighth kyu, which entitles you to wear a yellow belt. If you have some deficiencies in your technique, you may have a "B" after your grade, or 8B kyu. This indicates that you have made the grade, but have a few things to tidy up. If you are on the borderline between grades, a major consideration will be your training record and how hard you train. Students who put in the minimum amount of training time and effort cannot expect any serious consideration. Those who make maximum effort demonstrate that they have made as much progress as their bodies will allow, so the higher grade is appropriate.

chapter 20

tournaments and
demonstrations

The Purpose of the Tournament

ET'S CONSIDER an exciting part of karate training, the tournament. Karate organizations have differing views on tournaments, depending on their philosophy. Very traditional

Figure 20-1: Tournaments are an excellent way to test your abilities. Takamichi Maeshima (left) prepares to counter punch after avoiding a kick by Paul Drucker (right) at the East Coast Shotokan Karate Association Goodwill Tournament.

karate organizations usually do not believe in having tournaments at all, since they hold that karate is not a sport but a self-defense system. They feel that such tournaments depart from real karate training. However, most of the current traditional organizations do include tournaments as an additional method of training. Their philosophy goes something like this: The tournament is just another method of training. In the tournament, the competitor gets to test his technique against others with whom he does not usually train. This will help him to identify his own strong and weak points. Having done this in the tournament, he can then go back to the dojo to strengthen his deficiencies.

To illustrate this, let's consider the following. You enter the tournament and are called for your first match. You bow in, and the referee signals for the match to begin. As you face your opponent you see that his midsection is open. In spite of your best efforts, you cannot seem to score with your front kick. The lesson learned here is that you need more practice with your kick. Perhaps it fell short and you need to practice distancing. Perhaps your opponent shifted in and countered you before you could get the kick off. This might mean that your initial sparring distance was too close. You manage to win several matches, but in each one an opponent has scored on you using a kick to your lower body. This might indicate that your blocking needs improvement. These can be valuable lessons to learn, particularly as they relate to your ability to protect yourself. If a karate practitioner approaches the tournament with the idea that he or she is there to learn, not just to collect a trophy, then the tournament is a valuable training exercise. On the other hand, if your purpose in entering the tournament is just to win a trophy or title, you have crossed the line from martial arts to sports. Tournaments should be viewed as a type of training, not the reason for training.

We are considering the practice of karate as a lifelong endeavor. Tournaments are primarily for the young. Generally, fifty-year-old karate practitioners cannot keep up with those half their age. A look at any contemporary sport will demonstrate that this is true. The good news is that even the older practitioner can compete, but in a senior division. Usually this means those over the age of forty-five. The senior division does not usually include sparring, but focuses on kata. If you fall into the senior category, by all means attend the tournament and participate. Even if you do not win, the experience is great. It will provide you with a focus for your training, and you will be able to see what others your age have accomplished. There is nothing like comparing your techniques with others' to motivate you.

Full Contact or No Contact?

Tournaments are frequently advertised as being "No Contact" or "Full Contact" in nature. This can be misleading. Let's take a look at how tournaments have developed. In the early days of training, the emphasis was on kata, with no free-sparring at all. Prearranged sparring drills came into use, but they prohibited contact with the opponent. After World War II ended, the reorganization of karate caused it to head in a new direction, that of the sports contest. This was largely influenced by other sports such as kendo or judo, and rules were made up that were similar in nature for the sparring matches. Gymnastics and figure skating utilized a system by which judges determined the value of a performance and awarded points competitively, and this model was followed for kata competitions.

The major problem was how to conduct the sparring match without causing injury to the participants. Karate had been designed to cause serious damage to the opponent, so a forceful application of its arsenal would not be suitable for sports events. It was immediately determined that the most dangerous techniques could not be used in sports matches. These included attacks to the eyes, groin, and knee joints, where a mistake could cause serious injury or death. However, other techniques, although considered less dangerous, were still capable of causing fatal injuries. Various methods of competing safely

---

Some traditional karate organizations don't believe in having tournaments. However, many believe that tournaments are a great training method and way to test one's abilities.

---

were tried, all with their shortcomings. Bamboo body armor, similar to that used in kendo practice, was used, as well as heavily padded chest protectors, gloves, and helmets. Although the torso area could be protected from injury, kicks and punches to the head could still seriously injure a competitor, in spite of the headgear worn. Some of the organizations opted to allow full contact to the body armor, but no attacks at all to the head. Others allowed full contact to the body and attacks to the head that were pulled short of contact. Most of the styles went to the no-contact type of match, in which the technique is pulled just short of contact. This allowed the maximum use of a variety of techniques, even though they could not be carried to their conclusion.

Some organizations claim that they have full-contact matches. However, most do not allow punches or other hand techniques aimed at the head. None of the systems is perfect, but it is understood that they are adaptations needed to make the tournaments as safe as possible. Even the no-contact matches have their injuries, although they are kept to a minimum by good training and competent judges.

Organization Tournaments versus Open Tournaments

> There are two types of tournaments: open tournaments, which are open to anyone willing to pay the required fees, and organization tournaments, which are restricted to members of that organization.

Basically, there are two types of tournaments, those run by karate organizations for their own members and those run by promoters to make money. The former are restricted to members of the karate organization, while the latter allow anyone to enter who has paid the required fees. Let's compare the two.

Organizational Tournaments

As noted above, traditional karate organizations view tournaments as a type of training; therefore, participants are expected to behave as though they are in a dojo. In tournaments such as these, there is little conflict over the correct way to perform a kata or over the rules of the tournament. Participants concentrate on perfecting their techniques, not on trying to prove that their organization or karate style is superior. One of the features that makes these tournaments better than others is that the rules are usually written down. In order to judge, a black belt has to know the rule book and train to be a judge. This leaves little room for dispute over whether correct procedures have been carried out. These tournaments are usually run by, or at least overseen by, senior ranked instructors, so they are well organized and have few problems. Participants know that their entry fees, which are usually minimal, are helping their organization. The only downside is that in some organizations there may be little variety in the types of techniques used, since everyone trains in the same way. For instance, Shotokan practitioners are taught to advance against their opponent whenever possible. They look for the opening and then charge straight in. This makes it a bad idea to turn one's back to perform a back kick, since one might easily be scored upon. As a result, one does not see many back kicks in a Shotokan tournament. In some systems, the fighters more or less adopt stationary positions and throw one or two techniques and then step back. Under these circumstances, a back kick would not be so risky.

Let's look at a typical traditional karate tournament as run by the International Shotokan Karate Federation. This will be a regional tournament, with competitors from several states and a number of schools. It will usually begin on time, since preregistration is required, with a cutoff date for entries usually a week or two prior to the day of the tournament. This gives the tournament committee time to feed the names of the contestants into a computer program that puts forth a random list of match couplings and ring assignments. Upon arriving on the day of the tournament, contestants are assigned to compete in one of the rings and report there.

Judges have been assigned to rings as well. Each ring will have several senior judges who will act as referees, as well as junior judges who will occupy the seated positions in each corner. Overseeing each ring will be a senior instructor who will act as the arbitrator in case there is a question about the rules or procedure. If there is a dispute over any procedure in the competition ring, the team coach may approach the arbitrator and ask for a clarification. Only the arbitrator may stop a match. Coaches and contestants are forbidden to approach the judges, and only a coach may seek the arbitrator's council. Arbitrators may stop the match and confer with the judges, if they think there is a procedural issue that requires a decision. If there has been a violation of the rules, the judges will make the appropriate correction. Arbitrators may not challenge the judges' call under any circumstances. If the judges have decided that the technique is worth a point, then that is final.

Under these circumstances, contestants do their best and the tournament is under control. This leads to fewer injuries and a better training experience for the competitors. The judges in each ring, as well as the arbitrator, are under the supervision of the chief judge, who makes ring assignments and generally evaluates the performance of the judges. If judges are observed to consistently make poor calls, they may not be assigned to judge in the future but will be required to undergo further training until they improve.

Judges must complete a specific training program in order to be certified. They are ranked as A, B, C, or D judges, with A as the highest and D as the beginning stage. Promotion between the ranks is correlated with the belt rank and based on participation in the Instructor Training Program, as well as the passing of written and practical tests. In addition, there is a time requirement between the judges' ranks as well. In this manner, the judging is kept to a high quality.

Judges are responsible for the safety of contestants. If a contestant shows a lack of control and makes contact with his opponent, he may be given a warning, *chui*. Two warnings will constitute a foul, *hansoku,* and he will be disqualified. Serious contact, total disregard for the rules, disobeying the referee's directions, or other dangerous behavior or breach of the rules may be grounds for disqualifying a contestant as well. Contestants who are disqualified are usually banned from tournaments for a year. Under these conditions, contests are run safely and efficiently. Most of the major organizations have similar practices with written rules and judges' training as the norm.

A *chui* is a warning given by a judge to a contestant; two warnings constitute a *hansoku*, or a foul.

The tournament described above is a typical regional tournament, but other types of competitions may be held as well. Normally, in order to participate in a regional tournament where free-sparring is the norm, one must have achieved brown-belt rank. Sometimes smaller tournaments are run, and lower ranks are allowed to compete. For the beginners through purple belts, the sparring competition is one-step sparring. This keeps students focused on the important parts of training, which emphasize a solid foundation in basic techniques before advancing. It also keeps injuries to a minimum. It takes a great deal of skill and training to free-spar, and beginners attempting it frequently get injured.

Children's tournaments are run much the same way, but they are usually broken into categories according to age groups as well as belt ranks. This may prove to be a lot of work for the tournament director, since he will have to organize many competition ladders. In the early age groups, up to about ten years of age or so, boys and girls may compete in kata against one another. Above that age, separate competitions for boys and girls are usually the norm.

Promotional Tournaments

Now let's look at the open tournaments. In the early 1960s, a number of individuals began to run karate championships. Winners of these tournaments were given titles indicating that they were the regional, national, or international champions. The only problem was that there were many different tournaments run by different individuals, each granting such titles. In a short time, the titles lost their meaning. Trophies in these tournaments reached gigantic proportions, with some taller than the contestants who won them.

Two major problems were evident in these events. The first had to do with rules. Common sense dictates that if you are going to have a sports competition, the rules must be written down in a rule book. Sports familiar to Americans all have official rule books. Those who referee in baseball, football, and other sports must train to be referees, a process that requires them to know the rule book by heart and go through a training program to be certified. Since the open karate tournaments were run by individuals, there was no training of referees and no set of written rules. Meetings were held prior to the tournament, and all black belts were required to judge. This seems ridiculous, since we never see baseball players or other sports participants judge in the same game in which they are playing. Since there were no written rules and no judges who had trained with them, the judging in these tournaments was exceptionally bad. Points were awarded for poorly executed techniques, and the winner frequently was not the best contestant, simply the one who had learned how to exploit the situation to his advantage. In many cases, schools that had brought a large number of students to the contest could manipulate the promoter into overruling a judge's decision against them by threatening to pull their students from the competition and demand a refund.

Many of these tournaments were more like unorganized circuses than serious training experiences. The only thing one could count on was that the promoter was making money. For the serious karate practitioner, they were very frustrating.

Since there were no written rules and no judges trained in their use, injuries were common. Some schools with incompetent instructors attended these tournaments with an agenda, to legitimize the instructors' reputation. In order to do so, unnecessary contact was made, causing many injuries.

A second problem with these contests had to do with judging kata. In a traditional tournament run by a karate organization, judges would know all of the kata being performed and the correct way to perform them. Competitors would be judged according to their knowledge of the kata. In an open tournament, Shodans with only a few years training would be in the position of judging kata from other styles with which they were not familiar. This led to two additional problems. In an organization-run tournament, where everyone has to do the kata the same way, errors are easily picked up. In an open tournament a competitor could make a mistake or leave out a move and the judges would not know. Conceivably he could win a competition even though he should have lost.

Still another problem caused by the nonstandardized performance of kata in competition was the changing of traditional kata to include flashy moves designed to impress judges. I watched an open karate tournament many years ago in which a competitor performed the kata Kanku Dai. This kata has a jump kick at the end, as well as some side kicks and front kicks within the kata. Since the performer had good kicking ability, he added a couple of high kicks for good measure to impress the judges. It worked, since no one could question whether they rightfully belonged in the kata. If they had questioned him, he simply could have said that it was the way his style practiced that particular form. In this manner, many changes have taken place in traditional kata, not because they are better interpretations, but simply so that they will impress incompetent judges and win trophies.

An attempt to unify the karate movement came in the early 1970s with the formation of the World Union of Karate Organizations, or WUKO. This organization managed to bring together an international group of karate systems and also instituted judges' training and contest rules. They had some success in organizing regional, national, and international tournaments and probably had the most success of any of the organizations that tried to unify the karate movement.

Shortly thereafter, the Amateur Athletic Union, working in conjunction with Hidetaka Nishiyama's All American Karate Federation, accepted karate as an AAU sport, with an eye toward eventual participation in the Olympics. For the first year or two, AAU karate was under the control of the AAKF, which instituted written rules and judged training. Within a short time, the proliferation of styles included in the AAU tournaments led to difficulties in judging and controlling the competition practices. As a result, the AAU was not able to unify the American karate movement. The overall picture is that karate in the

United States is divided, with many schools participating in WUKO tournaments, AAU tournaments, and those hosted by other groups such as the International Traditional Karate Federation and the International Shotokan Karate
Federation. This lack of organization in American karate reflects the situation
throughout the world, making it difficult to gain acceptance for karate as an
Olympic sport.

seminars and
training camps

T RAINING CAMPS and seminars can be valuable experiences for those wishing to learn karate. Let's look at the seminar first.

Seminars

Seminars are usually one-day affairs, during which a particularly well-known instructor may be invited to teach a class or several classes. High-ranked instructors frequently tour the country, stopping in each region and giving a seminar. These seminars are usually arranged by organizations. For a reasonable fee, you are permitted to train in the class under such an expert. This is a good idea for several reasons. First of all, each instructor has a particular style of teaching and his own specialty. You may have spent much of your time with your primary teacher and have learned a great deal, but a visiting instructor can provide a different view of what you have been taught. Instructors have noted many instances in which their students trained with another in this type

Seminars are a great way to expand your understanding of karate technique and meet new training partners.

of seminar. In many cases, they came back and reported that the instructor told them that a particular technique of theirs needed correction, and had shown them some methods for doing it. This should have come as no surprise, since the things they reported were exactly the same things their regular instructor had told them over and over. Having heard it from someone else gave them a second opinion, one that somehow stuck.

One of my experiences in a seminar made me change my thinking about how to train. In the early 1980s, the Japan Karate Association's chief instructor, the late Master Masatoshi Nakayama, came to the Philadelphia area to teach a weekend seminar. We attended the special black-belt training, expecting to be taught all sorts of advanced techniques that were not in our normal repertoire. Instead, the emphasis for the weekend's classes was on basic hip movement, as the renowned master drilled us over and over on how to utilize correct hip movement in our karate technique. Without a complete understanding of the principles of correct hip placement, rotation, and snap, more advanced technique would never be possible. From that point on, many of us began to give greater thought to revisiting our basics, much to our benefit.

Other reasons for attending seminars are just as obvious. You may be part of a large karate organization, but your club may be located in an out-of-the-way place. Your organization may send some of its top instructors to various clubs so that they may have the benefit of training with them. Usually these training seminars will draw people from several clubs, so the added bonus is that you will have some new people to train with, which is always a positive experience. The downside of the seminar is that it is usually limited to a class or two, and you will have to wait for the next seminar to get additional instruction.

Training Camps

Training camps last anywhere from a weekend to a week. The larger ones may draw people from throughout the nation, or even have an international attendance. Since they are bigger, they may pull together top instructors from many areas and a large number of students. One of the best known of these is the Master Camp run by the International Shotokan Karate Federation. The camp is held in June each year at Camp Green Lane in Pennsylvania. At the 2002 camp, attended by over four hundred participants, were instructors from the United States and Canada. The chief instructor of the camp was world-renowned Ninth-Degree Master Teruyuki Okazaki. He was assisted by a battery of other instructors, including two Eighth Degrees, six Seventh Degrees, and two Sixth Degrees. In addition to drawing students from the United States and

Canada, the camp attracted groups came from Mexico, Israel, and a number of South and Central American countries.

Classes in such camps are usually divided into beginner, intermediate, and advanced, with training held three to four times a day. Special classes for instructor trainees are also given. These camps provide a good opportunity to get away from the problems of daily life and simply concentrate on learning

Training camps provide the opportunity to learn from top instructors.

the art. With so many top instructors and enthusiastic students at the camp, you cannot help but benefit. Many of the camps have provisions for enrolling for a limited number of days instead of staying a full week. Normally the fees for these camps are quite reasonable, particularly in light of the variety and quality of instruction.

chapter 22
becoming
an instructor

HERE ARE TWO ranking systems in many karate organizations. One speaks for your personal proficiency in karate and is recognized in the awarding of dan ranks. The other system is for those who have chosen to become instructors. Instructor, examiner, and judge ranks require additional training above and beyond the physical training demanded of regular practitioners.

As you advance through the ranks, you may reach a point where you wish to instruct others. This can be accomplished in a number of ways. Let's take the easy way first. We live in a free country, and you can hang out your shingle and teach karate at any stage in your training. It is not uncommon to see some individuals with only a slight knowledge of karate open schools, teach, and promote others. Since there is no central authority for regulating karate, this has taken place many times. Students promoted by these unqualified instructors can, at any time, open their own schools. In time, the quality of instruction and the level of proficiency goes completely downhill. This topic was discussed earlier, so we need not belabor the point. But how does one become a "real" instructor? What is the process?

To begin with, you will probably have to assist your instructor at some point, after you have trained for a couple of years. There will be times when he will need assistance, and you may be asked to show students how to do a basic block or lead them through a kata as they are learning it. These are valuable experiences, and you should be grateful for the opportunity to help. Trying to teach karate to another makes you look at things a little differently, and you will benefit from the experience. However, this does not mean that you are an instructor.

Like many organizations, the ISKF requires that all persons wanting to be a karate instructor must be twenty-two years of age, hold Sandan rank, and be recommended by their club's instructor before they can enter the two-year training program.

Most established karate organizations have procedures by which you can become a certified instructor. Usually this means that you have attained a minimum age and rank. For instance, the practices of the International Shotokan Karate Federation (ISKF) ensure that instructors are at least twenty-four years of age and hold Sandan rank before they are certified.

Let's once again take a look at the ISKF program as a guide. The ISKF Instructor Training Institute is held at several of its regional headquarters: Philadelphia, New Orleans, Denver, Fort Lauderdale, and Phoenix. Prospective instructor trainees must be at least twenty-two years of age and be recommended by their club's instructor. Prior to completing the course, they must pass the Sandan exam. The course requires full-time participation for a two-year period, and the instructor trainee will work as an assistant instructor in the headquarters. For those not able to devote two years full-time, the course may be completed as a part-time program, which will take much longer. This is usually acceptable for instructors who have their own schools and are teaching on a daily basis. Lengthy training sessions are held at the headquarters one weekend a month, and trainees are expected to attend the Master Camp and the fall camp, where they take special classes taught by the top instructors.

In addition to the actual training, the prospective instructors must write forty-three research papers on varied subjects dealing with the history and philosophy of karate, as well as papers on kinesiology, kata, fighting techniques, and various physiological and psychological subjects relating to karate. During their period of enrollment, trainees are also required to attend all tournaments hosted by the organization, including children's and collegiate tournaments. There they practice their judging. They must also attend examinations in order to learn the fine points of examining students for various ranks. Although they are permitted to sit on the examining board and participate in the discussions, they have no vote until they graduate. After they have attended the required number of instructor trainee classes and have completed their papers, they must also pass practical and written exams for certification as an official instructor, examiner, and tournament judge. This process ensures that they know their subject well enough to teach it and that their evaluation of students during exams will be in keeping with organization standards. It also ensures that they will be competent tournament judges.

We have discussed the ISKF practices for certifying instructors, and most of the large organizations operate in the same manner. If you are looking for a school, it is always a good idea to find out how the instructor trained for his role. Winning contests makes you a good competitor, but not necessarily a good instructor. Many of our best athletic coaches were not top players but have a special grasp of the principles of their sport and a unique ability to pass that information on to others.

resources

A TRIP TO THE LOCAL BOOKSTORE will reveal the large number of books published on the art of karate. Many are excellent, but others are not so good. The list below is to be considered representative of the better ones. It would be impossible to detail here the many fine karate books that have been written in English over the past half century.

Finding a book on the style that interests you is not necessarily an easy task. Some styles have no books about them published at all, while others have published works that, while excellent, have long been out of print. These may be found online through used-book dealers, although their price may be a bit high. Perhaps the easiest works to find are those about Shotokan karate. Numerous instructors have published works over the years, and Shotokan is perhaps the best covered of all the karate systems. Also included in the list below are some periodicals that cover traditional karate. Of the many on the newsstand, these will give the reader the best overview. Books about other martial arts, such as those of Chinese origin or the Korean systems, are not included here, since this work is about Okinawan/Japanese karate, but such books do exist on the market.

In the past decade or two, still another source of knowledge has been developed, the video. These are numerous and have been produced by practitioners of many styles. They usually show basics as well as many of the kata practiced in the system. The periodicals listed below have advertisements for many videotapes that will assist you in learning more about a particular system.

Books

Bishop, Mark. *Okinawan Karate Teachers, Styles, and Secret Techniques*. London: A & C Black Publishers, Ltd., 1991. Bishop has trained extensively on Okinawa for a number of years and has visited most of the dojos and masters on the island. He gives an excellent overview of present-day karate systems on the island as well as their historical development. If the reader is interested in practicing any of the Okinawan-based styles, this book is essential reading.

Bowerbank, Andres. *The Spirit of Karate-Do: Teachings of Masami Tsuruoka*. Toronto: Morris Marketing and Media Services, 1998. Masami Tsuruoka is the leading authority on Chito Ryu karate in North America and has trained many students, a number of whom have become instructors in their own right. This book presents his ideas and methods.

Cook, Harry. *Shotokan Karate: A Precise History*. England: By the author, 2001. Cook's work is the most detailed history of Shotokan karate yet undertaken. For any practitioner of Shotokan it is an extremely important book.

Demura, Fumio. *Shito Ryu Karate*. Valencia, CA: Black Belt Communications, Inc., 1971. Fumio Demura is perhaps the best-known exponent of Shito Ryu karate in the United States. In this work, he presents the elements of the style.

Dollar, Alan, and Robert Davidson, eds., and Alice Dollar, illus. *Secrets of Uechi Ryu Karate: And the Mysteries of Okinawa*. Cherokee, OK: Cherokee Publishing, 1996. Uechi Ryu karate is not widely practiced in the United States, and few books have been written about it. This work, coupled with that of George Mattson, should give the interested student an excellent overview of the style.

Draeger, Donn F. and Robert W. Smith. *Asian Fighting Arts*. Tokyo: Kodansha International Ltd., 1969. The late Donn Draeger was one of the most respected Western practitioners of martial arts in Japan. In this work the authors give an excellent description of the variety of martial arts practiced in the Far East.

Fraguas, Jose M. *Karate Masters*. Burbank, CA: Unique Publications Inc., 2001. Jose Fraguas presents a number of interviews with top experts in various styles of karate in the United States. Included among them are American and Asian practitioners.

Funakoshi, Gichin. *Karate Jutsu: The Original Teachings of Master Funakoshi*. Trans. by John Teramoto. Tokyo: Kodansha International Ltd., 2001. This is a modern translation of one of Gichin Funakoshi's early works on Shotokan. It includes photos of the legendary master performing various kata.

Funakoshi, Gichin. *Karate-Do Kyohan: The Master Text*. Trans. By Tsutomo Oshima. Tokyo: Kodansha International Ltd., 1973. This is Gichin Funakoshi's most complete work on the subject of Shotokan karate. Translated by karate master Tsutomu Oshima, it details the early practice of Shotokan, prior to World War II.

Funakoshi, Gichin. *Karate-Do: My Way of Life*. Tokyo: Kodansha International, 1975. This is the autobiography of Gichin Funakoshi. It is particularly valuable for insights into his philosophy of the martial arts, as well as the history of the development of his system.

Funakoshi, Gichin. *Karate-Do Nyumon: The Master Introductory Text*. Trans. by John Teramoto. Tokyo: Kodansha International Ltd., 1988. This is a modern translation of the introductory text by Master Funakoshi. It includes a number of photographs of his son and other prominent karate masters in action.

Funakoshi, Gichin. *To-Te Jitsu*. Hamilton, Canada: Masters Publications, 1997. This is a modern translation of another of Gichin Funakoshi's early works and includes photos of the master performing kata movements.

Haines, Bruce A. *Karate's History and Traditions*. Rutland, VT: Charles E. Tuttle Co., Publishers, 1968. Bruce Haines's work was the first attempt at a complete history of karate to be published in the West. It gives excellent insights into the development of karate, particularly in its transmission to the West.

Higaonna, Morio. *The History of Karate: Goju Ryu*. Thousand Oaks, CA: Dragon Books, 1995. Morio Higaonna is one of the best known of the modern masters of Goju Ryu karate. He presents the history of the style in great detail. This is an important work for all exponents of the style as well as for prospective students.

Hisataka, Masayuki. *Scientific Karatedo*. Tokyo: Japan Publications Trading Company, 1976. Shorinjiryu Kenkokan Karatedo is a little known style that was founded in the aftermath of World War II. It is quite different from many of the standard systems practiced in Japan today, and this work gives an excellent overview of the system.

Mattson, George E. *The Way of Karate*. Boston: Charles E. Tuttle Co., Inc., 1963. George Mattson wrote the first book on Uechi Ryu karate to be published in the West. It is a well-illustrated technical manual.

McCarthy, Pat and Mike Lee. *Classical Kata of Okinawan Karate*. Los Angeles: Ohara Publications, Inc., 1995. Pat McCarthy presents a number of the traditional kata of Okinawan karate in this work. It should be of interest to all practitioners of Okinawan-based karate systems.

Miki, Minobu. *Karate Shito Ryu: Advanced Kata*. Burbank, CA: Unique Publications Inc., 2001. Minobu Miki is a well-known master of Shito Ryu karate and has a large following in the United States. Here he presents the advanced kata of Shito Ryu.

Nagamine, Shoshin. *The Essence of Okinawan Karate-Do*. Boston: Charles E. Tuttle Co., Inc., 1976. Shoshin Nagamine is one of the best known of the Okinawan Shorin Ryu masters. Here he presents his philosophy and a history of the style. A major feature of the book is a detailed, well-illustrated series of the kata of Shorin Ryu as demonstrated by the master.

Nagamine, Shoshin. *Tales of Okinawa's Great Masters*. Trans. by Patrick McCarthy. Boston: Tuttle Martial Arts, 1998. In this work, Shoshin Nagamine reveals tales of the legendary masters of Okinawan karate.

Nakayama, Masatoshi. *Dynamic Karate*. Tokyo: Kodansha International Ltd., 1966. The late Masatoshi Nakayama, chief instructor of the Japan Karate Association, has published nearly twenty books on the subject of Shotokan karate. This is his master work, and it provides the most detailed analysis on the performance of karate movements yet undertaken. It is probably the most useful karate manual for any karate practitioner, regardless of style.

Nishiyama, Hidetaka and Richard C. Brown. *Karate: The Art of "Empty Hand" Fighting*. Boston: Charles E. Tuttle Co., Inc., 1961. Hidetaka Nishiyama's book broke new ground in the late 1950s when it was published. It has been continuously in print since that time, attesting to its excellence. For practitioners of Shotokan, as well as other styles, it presents an excellent overview of karate.

Okazaki, Teruyuki and Milorad V. Stricevic. *The Textbook of Modern Karate*. Tokyo: Kodansha International/USA Ltd., 1984. This is a very important work by Shotokan karate master Teruyuki Okazaki and sports physician Milorad Stricevic. Stricevic presents the results of exhaustive study of karate practitioners from a medical standpoint, showing the effects of various types of practice on the human body. The bulk of the book is a detailed analysis of karate movements presented Okazaki.

Oyama, Masatatsu. *Mas Oyama's Essential Karate*. New York: Sterling Publications Company Inc., 1978. This is an overall introductory text to the Kyokushinkai system, encompassing basics, sparring drills and kata, as well as supplementary training exercises.

Oyama, Masatatsu. *This Is Karate*. Tokyo: Japan Publications Trading Company, 1965. Masatatsu Oyama, founder of Kyokushinkai karate, presents a detailed overview of his style, including basics, kata, and sparring. For those wishing to learn more about Kyokushinkai, this is the manual to read.

Rielly, Robin L. *Complete Shotokan Karate: The Samurai Legacy and Modern Practice*. Boston: Charles E. Tuttle Co., Inc., 1998. The author provides an overview of the development of Shotokan karate and links it to the traditions of early modern Japan in order to further an understanding of the genesis of modern karate training. Considered to be two books in one, with the second half presenting a number of sparring drills and kata. This work was undertaken to help Westerners understand the cultural traditions behind modern karate.

Rielly, Robin L. *The Secrets of Shotokan Karate*. Boston: Charles E. Tuttle Co., Inc., 2000. The author presents insights into the various practices in Shotokan karate and identifies the essential elements of movement as they apply to sparring and kata. It is recommended for those who are beginning karate, as well as experienced practitioners.

Schmidt, Stan and Randall G. Hassell. *Meeting Myself: Beyond the Spirit of the Empty Hand*. St. Louis, MO: Palmoroton & Reed Publishing Company, 1997. Stan Schmidt is the highest-ranking Western master in the Japan Karate Association. His experiences training in Japan over a number of years are fascinating to read and help the reader to understand the differences between Westerners and Japanese.

Suzuki, Tatsuo. *Karate-Do*. London: Pelham Books Ltd., 1967. Tatsuo Suzuki is one of the highest-ranked Wado Ryu practitioners. In this work he presents the basics of the style, including sparring and kata.

Toguchi, Seikichi. *Okinawan Goju Ryu: Fundamentals of Shorei-Kan Karate*. Los Angeles: Ohara Publications, 1995. Seikichi Toguchi is one of the most senior masters of Goju Ryu karate. Here he presents his views on the performance of Goju Ryu, including detailed instructions on various training methods.

Yamaguchi, Gosei. *The Fundamentals of Goju-Ryu*. Danville, CA: Goju-Kai Karate Do, U.S.A., 1972. Gosei Yamaguchi, son of the famous Goju Ryu master Gogen Yamaguchi, details the basics of the style as practiced in Japan.

Yamakura, Motoo. *Goju-Ryu Karate-Do: Fundamentals for Traditional Practitioners, Vol 1*. San Francisco: Goju-Ryu Karate-Do Kyokai, 2000. Motoo Yamakura's work is devoted to explaining the basics of Goju Ryu karate for beginners, as well as more advanced practitioners.

Periodicals

American Samurai
P.O. Box 866
Cary City, NC 27512
www.AmericanSamurai.com

Dragon Times
Dragon Associates, Inc.
P.O. Box 6039
Thousand Oaks, CA 91359
818-889-3856
www.dragon-tsunami.org

The Journal of Asian Martial Arts
Via Media Publishing
821 W. 24th St.
Erie, PA 16502
800-455-9517
www.goviamedia.com

Shotokan Karate Magazine
S.K.M.
P.O. Box 53, Lymm, Cheshire,
WA13OHH.
United Kingdom
www.zee.com/skmn/index.php

glossary

A

Age-uke: Rising block

Age-zuki: Rising punch

Awase-zuki: U-punch

B

Bunkai: Practical application of kata moves

C

Choku-zuki: Straight punch

Chudan: Midsection

Chui: Warning (match terminology)

D

Dan: Black-belt ranks

Dojo: Training hall

E

Empi: Elbow

Empi-uchi: Elbow strike

En-sho: Round heel

F

Fudo-dachi: Rooted stance

Fumikomi: Stomping kick

G

Gaiwan: Outer arm

Gaiwan-gedan-uke: Lower sweeping block

Gedan: Lower area of the body

Gedan-barai: Downward sweeping block

Gi: Training uniform

Gohon-kumite: Five-step sparring

Gyaku-zuki: Reverse punch

H

Hachiji-dachi: Open-leg stance

Haishu: Back-hand

Haito: Ridge-hand

Haito-uchi: Ridge-hand strike

Haiwan: Back-arm

Hajime: Begin

Hangetsu-dachi: Half-moon stance

Hangetsu Kata: Kata from the Shorei tradition

Hanmi: Half-front facing position

Hansoku: Foul (match terminology)

Hasami-zuki: Scissors punch

Heian: Series of kata, also called Pinan

Heiko-dachi: Parallel stance

Heisoku-dachi: Informal-attention stance

Hidari: Left

Hiraken: Fore-knuckle fist

Hiraken-zuki: Fore-knuckle fist punch

Hizagashira: Kneecap

I

Ippon: One point (match terminology)

Ippon-ken: One-knuckle fist

Ippon-ken-zuki: One-knuckle punch

Ippon-kumite: One-step sparring

Ippon-nukite: One-finger spear-hand

J

Jiyu-ippon-kumite: One-point free-sparring

Jiyu-kamae: Free-sparring stance

Jiyu-kumite: Free-sparring

Jodan: Face area

Jodan-age-uke: Upper-level block

Jogai: Outside the ring (match terminology)

Juji-uke: X-block

K

Kage-zuki: Hook punch

Kaisho: Open-hand

Kakato: Heel

Kakuto: Bent wrist

Kamae-te: Command to assume a fighting position

Kanku-Dai: Kata from the Shorin tradition

Kanku-Sho: Kata from the Shorin tradition

Karate: Empty hand

Karate-ka: A karate practitioner

Kata: Formal exercises

Keage: Snap-kick

Keito: Chicken-head wrist

Kekomi: Thrust-kick

Kentsui: Hammer-fist

Kentsui-uchi: Hammer-fist strike

Keri: Kick

Keri-waza: Kicking techniques

Kiba-dachi: Straddle stance

Kihon-kumite: Basic sparring

Kizami-zuki: Jab

Kokutsu-dachi: Back stance

Koshi: Ball of the foot

Kumade: Bear-hand

Kumite: Sparring

Kyu: Ranks below black belt

M

Maai: Distancing

Mae-ashi-mae-geri: Front kick using the front foot

Mae-geri: Front kick

Mae-geri-keage: Front snap-kick

Mae-geri-kekomi: Front thrust-kick

Mae-tobi-geri: Front jumping kick

Makiwara: Punching post

Mawashi-geri: Roundhouse kick

Mawashi-zuki: Roundhouse punch

Migi: Right

Mikazuki-geri: Crescent kick

Mokuso: Command to meditate

Mokuso-yame: Command to cease meditation

Morote-uke: Augmented forearm block

Morote-zuki: Double punch

Musubi-dachi: Informal attention stance with the feet turned out

N

Naore: Command to return to the informal attention stance, usually given at the end of an exercise

Nagashi-uke: Sweeping block

Naihanchi: Series of kata, also known as Tekki

Naha: A city in southern Okinawa that gave rise to one of the three major karate traditions

Naiwan: Inner arm

Nagashi-zuki: Sweeping punch

Nakadaka-ippon-ken: Middle-finger one-knuckle fist

Nakadaka-ken: Middle-finger knuckle-fist

Neko-ashi-dachi: Cat-foot stance

Nidan geri: Double jump-kick

Nihon-nukite: Two-finger spear-hand

Nukite: Spear-hand

O

Oi-zuki: Lunge punch

R

Rei: Bow

Renoji-dachi: L stance

Renzoku-geri: Combination kicks

S

Sanchin-dachi: Hourglass stance

Sanbon-kumite: Three-step sparring

Seiken: Fore-fist

Seiken-zuki: Fore-fist punch

Seiryuto: Ox-jaw hand

Sensei: Teacher

Seiza: Meditation position

Shiko-dachi: Square stance

Shittsui: Knee-hammer

Shizentai: Natural position

Shuri: A city in southern Okinawa that gave rise to a major karate tradition

Shuto: Knife-hand

Shuto-uchi: Knife-hand strike

Shuto-uke: Knife-hand block

Sochin-dachi: Diagonal straddle-leg stance (also called Fudo-dachi)

Sokuto: Side edge of the foot

Soto-uke: Outside block

T

Tate-shuto-uke: Vertical knife-hand block

Tate-zuki: Vertical-fist punch

Teiji-dachi: T stance

Teisho: Palm-heel

Teisho-uchi: Palm-heel strike

Teisho-uke: Palm-heel block

Tobi-geri: Jumping kick

Tokui-kata: Favorite kata

Tokui-waza: Favorite technique

Tomari: A city in southern Okinawa that gave rise to a major karate tradition

Tsumasaki: Tips of the toes

U

Uchi: Strike

Uchi-hachiji-dachi: Inverted open-leg stance

Uchi-uke: Inside block

Ude: Forearm

Ude-uke: Forearm block

Ura-zuki: Close punch

Uraken: Back-fist

Uraken-uchi: Back-fist strike

Ushiro-geri: Back kick

W

Wan: Arm

Washide: Eagle-hand

Wazari: One-half point (match terminology)

Y

Yama-zuki: Wide U-punch

Yame: Stop

Yoko-geri-keage: Side snap-kick

Yoko-tobi-geri: Side jump-kick

Yoko-geri-kekomi: Side thrust-kick

Yonhon-nukite: Four-finger spear-hand

Z

Zenkutsu-dachi: Front stance

ABOUT TUTTLE
"Books to Span the East and West"

Our core mission at Tuttle Publishing is to create books which bring people together one page at a time. Tuttle was founded in 1832 in the small New England town of Rutland, Vermont (USA). Our fundamental values remain as strong today as they were then—to publish best-in-class books informing the English-speaking world about the countries and peoples of Asia. The world has become a smaller place today and Asia's economic, cultural and political influence has expanded, yet the need for meaningful dialogue and information about this diverse region has never been greater. Since 1948, Tuttle has been a leader in publishing books on the cultures, arts, cuisines, languages and literatures of Asia. Our authors and photographers have won numerous awards and Tuttle has published thousands of books on subjects ranging from martial arts to paper crafts. We welcome you to explore the wealth of information available on Asia at **www.tuttlepublishing.com**.

OTHER MARTIAL ARTS TITLES TO ENJOY

KARATE
The Art of "Empty Hand" Fighting
Hidetaka Nishiyama and
Richard C. Brown
over 1,000 b&w photos
7 x 10 256 pp
$24.95 pb ISBN: 978-0-8048-1668-7

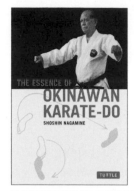

**THE ESSENCE OF OKINAWAN
KARATE-DO**
Shoshin Nagamine
over 1,000 b&w photos
6 x 9 280 pp
$19.95 pb ISBN: 978-0-8048-2110-0

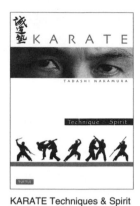

KARATE Techniques & Spirit
Tadashi Nakamura
over 700 b&w illus and
16 pp color insert
8.25 X 12 168 pp
$18.95 pb ISBN: 978-0-8048-3282-3

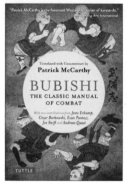

THE BIBLE OF KARATE BUBISHI
Patrick McCarthy
250 illus
6 x 9 216 pp
$18.95 pb ISBN: 978-4-8053-1384-8

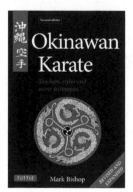

OKINAWAN KARATE
*Its Teachers, Styles, and
Secret Techniques*
Mark Bishop
100 b&w photos,
54 line drawings & charts, 1 map
6 x 9 206 pp
$16.95 pb ISBN: 978-0-8048-3205-2

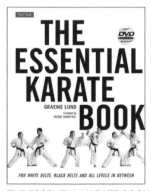

THE ESSENTIAL KARATE BOOK
*For White Belts, Black Belts and
all levels in between*
Graeme Lund
includes 32-minute DVD,
over 300 color photos and
over 200 b&w diagrams
6 x 9 208 hc
$16.95 pb ISBN: 978-4-8053-1297-1

* PRICES ARE SUBJECT TO CHANGE
For a complete listing of all MARTIAL ARTS books,
visit our website at www.tuttlepublishing.com